Coaching Millions

Help More People

Make More Money

Live Your Ultimate Lifestyle

By Milana Leshinsky

A special warm thanks to my mom and dad, my husband and my two children, my brother, my wonderful clients, and the whole cast of *"Friends"* – you kept me going when times got tough!

To my dear friends and mentors who influenced me or were directly responsible for my success:

Ramon Williamson, David Frey, Will Craig, Larina Kase, Kathy Sparks, and Angee Robertson.

To all the people who were my inspiration and support:

Thomas Leonard, Ken Evoy, Seth Godin, Michael Gerber, Soni Dimond, T. Harv Eker, Dan Kennedy, Michael Port, Andrea Lee, C.J. Hayden, Michael and Dawn Angier, Anthony Blake, Lia Allen, Tammy Burke, Lorraine Calhoun, Sterling Valentine, Chris Barrow, Fred Gleek, Terri Levine, Marlon Sanders, Donald Trump, Alex Mandossian, Joel Christopher, Travis Greenlee, Suzanne Falter-Barns, Wanda Loskot, Daniel Pink, Inna Panchenko.

Table of Contents

Foreword

Years ago, I read an interesting story about two young men:

> *"On a beautiful late spring afternoon, twenty five years ago, two young men graduated from the same college. They were very much alike. Both had been better than average students, both were personable and both—as young college graduates are—were filled with ambitious dreams for the future.*
>
> *Recently, these men returned to their college for their 25th reunion.*
>
> *They were still very much alike. Both were happily married. Both had three children. And both, it turned out, had gone to work for the same company after graduation, and where still there.*
>
> *But there was a difference. One of the men was manager of a small department of that company. The other was its president."*

Have you ever wondered, as I have, what makes this kind of difference in people's lives? It isn't always native intelligence or talent or dedication. It isn't that one person wants success and the other doesn't.

The difference lies in what each person knows, and how he or she makes use of that knowledge.

In *Coaching Millions*, Milana Leshinsky brilliantly illustrates this difference in coaches.

I can tell you without that reservation that when it comes to understanding the business of coaching, she is without peer.
I know this because I have enjoyed the opportunity of closely observing her extraordinary success over the past three years and, because the principles and strategies she teaches here are the very same that have proven effective in my own business and life for more than two decades.

With that said, I am humbled to be asked to compose the foreword to a book that will surely be regarded as a seminal work in the field.

Whether you are a new or experienced coach, a coach in training or an entrepreneur seeking to integrate coaching into your present work, *Coaching Millions* is required reading.

From choosing a profitable niche to coaching products to passive revenue, *Coaching Millions* offers a step-by-step blueprint along with the necessary thinking for success.

That's why I enthusiastically endorse and commend this book to the worldwide coaching community as an invaluable resource worthy of diligent study and application.

If you're reading this foreword before purchasing the book, here are three very good reasons to buy it now:

(1) First, this information is experience-based, experience-tested and experience-proven, in the author's business as well as my own;

(2) Second, applying what you learn here will save you years of trial and error, wasted effort and unnecessary frustration; and

(3) Third, it's a bargain—the cover price should be at least $1,000.

If you have already purchased it, resolve now to put this book into action. Here are two "coaching" notes to help:

1) If you're like most people, including me, you probably approach non-fiction books with the intention of gaining specific information. And because *Coaching Millions* is intended to be applied in a synergistic way, I urge you to resist the temptation to skim the table of contents and jump ahead to topics that interest you most. Instead, start from the beginning, complete the exercises as you go along and consider working privately with a coach or joining a group program to accelerate your results.

2) You may also be tempted to skip over or even ignore some of the advice you read here because it doesn't fit in with your particular "stream," brand or approach to coaching. Again, I urge you to resist this temptation, and I invite you to give yourself permission to travel outside of your current level of thinking and way of operating to fully experience the business, income and life transformation available to you inside.

An old Indian adage says: "When the student is ready the teacher appears."

If you're ready to help more people, make more money and enjoy your ultimate lifestyle as a coaching entrepreneur, I can think of no better "teacher" than the book you are holding in your hands.

Once you have applied the ideas here, I'm certain you will agree.

With love and respect,

Ramon Williamson

June 2007

Preface

The lowest point in my life happened in March of 1993. I was living in Syracuse, New York, and the entire East Coast was under a heavy blizzard. This was my first year in the U.S. I had no car, no money, and no job. I was 19, and piano lessons for six dollars an hour was the only opportunity open to me at that time. No blizzard could stop me from walking a couple of miles to a music store, where my student would be waiting for me.

I walked through through piles of snow, with freezing wind in my face and my boots sinking in the snow to the point where I couldn't feel my feet. When I finally reached the store, I received a message from the student's dad saying that she couldn't make it.

I felt like I was Scarlett O'Hara from "Gone With the Wind." Clenching my teeth, I walked back to my apartment and swore that I would do everything in my power to never need the six dollars that bad again. Of course, I didn't have a dirty old carrot in my hand, and I wasn't planning to "steal, lie or cheat..." But I was very determined to get out of the rut.

Since then, I became an adult, attended three colleges, had both of my children, and became an entrepreneur. If only I had known the amazing journey that was ahead of me!

Needless to say, I feel very biased toward this country. I couldn't have dreamt the life it allowed me to create, even in my wildest dreams growing up in Kiev, Ukraine. I am always puzzled to see so many people struggle here when the success is right there in front of them. Just reach out and grab it, it's yours!

Taxes and bureaucracy aside, there is an amazing freedom of choices here. Are there obstacles? Of course! But there is one thing that always keeps me going—burning desire. It's like somebody pushed a "start" button in my brain that cold and blustery day, and there is no way of stopping me.

This burning desire is the number one factor that makes people succeed. The biography of every successful entrepreneur is proof of that. Just read about Thomas Edison or Milton Hershey. There is no way someone would be willing to fail dozens—or hundreds!—of times just to find a concept that worked, unless they were driven by burning desire.

So the question is, do you have it? Do you have this gut-wrenching, stomach-turning feeling inside of you that pulls you forward? Do you ever get this nauseating feeling when you see someone else come out with a great product or business idea, and you turn "green" because you didn't think of it first?

Going from six dollars an hour to multi-six figures doesn't require previous business experience or Harvard degree—in fact, I had neither. All you need is the *thirst* for success—everything else is just mechanics.

Of course, having a guide, your personal "expedition leader," will give you a great advantage. As your guide, I will show you many shortcuts you can take and hundreds of mistakes you can avoid.

What I ask of you is a single-minded commitment for the next 3-6 months. Focus entirely on building a business of your dreams. This goal must become more important to you than any others. Summon all of your energy to make it happen. Resist any distraction that may sidetrack you from your ultimate goal.

That is how success is born, and it will be well worth it!

Part I
Coaching - The Business of Solving Problems

"An entrepreneur is nothing more than a problem solver."
— *T. Harv Eker, Secrets of the Millionaire Mind*

What Is Coaching?

Like many entrepreneurs, I launched my business with an idea, very little cash, and even less experience. As a recent immigrant from Ukraine, I was equipped with a background in classical music, English as a second language, and an ex-Soviet's knowledge of how to succeed in a capitalist economy. In other words, I was clueless.

Every step forward was a trial; every other step was an error. I started out as a web developer and an Internet marketing consultant. Most clients were willing to pay just enough to allow me to buy groceries. I lowered my prices to attract new clients, but this only lured "low-quality" clients–demanding, knit-picky people who called me at all hours of the day and night.

I struggled for months, reading books, attending seminars, posting questions on message boards, and working countless hours. My simple goal was to earn a decent income. Some people say, "I know what to do; I just need to do it." Well, looking back today, I realize that I didn't even know what to do!

I was introduced to the coaching industry by two coaches who purchased my web design product. (It was pure chance: it could have been two accountants, organizers, or real estate agents.) They were looking for a way to build their web site on a budget, and my do-it-yourself tutorial was just what they needed.

There must have been something in that tutorial or on my web site, because a few weeks later they invited me to join their coaching team as an Internet Business coach. I had no idea what coaching was but if they thought that I was a good fit for them, I was not going to disagree. I became the fourth coach on a team, consisting of a life coach, a parenting coach and a legal coach.

The team quickly dissolved due to poor planning, but it affected the direction of my business in ways I could never have imagined. Before I knew it, I was running a worldwide online organization for hundreds of coaches, rubbing shoulders with top experts in the field, and working closely with some of the most masterful coaches and veterans of the industry.

I started noticing a very interesting thing in coaching businesses–there was a huge gap between coaches desperately struggling to get a couple of paying clients *and* coaches who thrive and make six to seven figures a year working in similar target markets. Some would leave coaching and decide to get a job, while others would go on to become best-selling authors, celebrated experts and leaders in their field.

Coaching can be one of the most lucrative service professions in the world, with rates ranging from $75 to $350 per hour. Although today, only one in ten coaches earn an annual six-figure income. Industry-wide, 34% of professionals make $25,000 to $50,000, and 26% earn $10,000 or less. Only 4% of coaches reported earning more than $175,000! The median annual income for a coach is $37,500[1].

After much research, observation, personal experience, and working with hundreds of coaches over the years, I began making some revelations about why this is happening. It all started making sense.

Why are there so many low-income professionals? Here is what I've observed over the years. Most business and life coaches focus on *finding clients* and on the *coaching process* itself. They attend one networking meeting after another, handing out business cards, asking for referrals, schmoozing–doing anything to broadcast to the world, "I'm accepting new coaching clients!" Using this approach, it usually takes several years to build a practice that pays a living wage, and by that point, many coaches have given up.

What about those who stay in business and prosper?

Approximately 9% of would-be coaches become high-income "coaching entrepreneurs" and celebrities. These coaches enjoy low-stress, high-reward lifestyles that are the envy of their neighbors. They feel little pressure to find new clients and no stress if a particular client leaves. These coaches are not anxious clock-watchers. Instead, they awake each morning feeling excited about the new day.

Best of all, coaching entrepreneurs have no income limit. They can generate as much as $500,000 to several million dollars per year, and their earnings have nothing to do with how many clients they have or how many hours they work.

---

[1] Coaching Practices, California School of Organizational Studies at Alliant International University.

Being a coaching entrepreneur means creating solutions to your target clients' problems. These solutions are not only limited to the coaching process: They include tools, programs, software, events, books, consulting, and other products and services that will help your clients solve a problem or achieve a goal.

What is Coaching?

After working closely with coaches, trainers and consultants on many different levels, running an online coaching community, and organizing annual worldwide coaching telesummits, here's what I know: Coaching is a methodology–a strategy used by thousands of people worldwide to inspire, motivate, and evoke positive change in the lives of others.

A coach is anyone who inspires to take action and provides a "back-end" strategy that facilitates success. If this sounds too academic, let me say it in a more simple way: whether you speak, train, consult or write, you can offer coaching to help your clients and customers succeed.

Coaching is a tool or approach used to solve a problem or reach a goal. It needs to be mastered through training, experience, or both. It's just ONE approach. There are many others.

Once you understand that coaching is simply a tool, you will focus on *solving problems,* the primary reason clients want to work with you.

Nobody cares about the coaching process itself until it brings tangible results. You'll be able to create a multitude of solutions for your clients, build a REAL sustainable business, and become a leading coach in your field.

Practitioners vs. Entrepreneurs

With Scottish newspapers calling us "fortune tellers" and "friends for hire," and thousands of coaches struggling to attract clients, I couldn't wait to write this book! Coaching has been surrounded by misconceptions for years.

In the next few years, two types of coaches will clearly emerge: *Practitioners* and *Entrepreneurs*.

Practitioners will be offering coaching as the primary "product" in their business. They will charge clients hourly or monthly fees, and their goal will be to fill their practice. Because their income is tightly connected to their time, there will always be some limitations to how much their business can grow.

Entrepreneurs, on the other hand, will not sell coaching. Instead, they will *create a need for coaching* by inspiring and informing their customers in their area of expertise. They will sell products, training, seminars, and tools first, then offer coaching as a way to supporting their customers further. Their business model will be full of leverage and offer unlimited income growth.

Until now, nobody has developed a formula for becoming a highly successful *coaching entrepreneur*. In this book, I will reveal *six steps* to building a thriving business–one that offers the freedom to do what you love while creating real wealth for yourself and your family.

I will not only reveal to you how to get more clients than you ever need, but I will also show you how you can be viewed as the number one coach in your field. By the time you're finished reading this book, you'll be ready to become one of the most influential coaches in your industry.

Regardless of whether you're an established coach, or just getting started, I will help you uncover new profit centers that will dramatically improve your life for many years to come.

The information in this book is not only based on my professional and personal experience, but on the experiences of dozens of coaching entrepreneurs I interviewed during the last five years. In addition, I've conducted various surveys of more than 2,550 coaches, gaining tremendous insight into the "anatomy" of a successful coaching company.

My mission and purpose with this book is to reveal this path to you, step by step. My goal is to completely re-wire your thinking and turn you from a mid-level (or struggling) coach into a highly paid in-demand coaching entrepreneur.

Six Steps To Becoming A Coaching Entrepreneur

1. Choose a Coaching Niche

2. Pick Your Coaching Model

3. Build Your Market Presence

4. Develop Passive Income Sources

5. Create a Self-Propelled Lifestyle Business

6. Become a Leader in Your Niche

Everything I teach in this book has been tested and proven to work for me personally, as well as for many coaches with whom I worked, partnered, and interviewed. It is based on the articles, notes, coaching sessions and experiences I compiled over the years, and comes with an action guide which gives you specific steps to help you achieve amazing results.

I am also going to show you how you can build a business that works without you. Whether you decide to stop coaching in the future, open a second business, or ultimately sell your coaching company for a lot of money, you will be equipped with the right knowledge and systems to accomplish this.

Most people still don't know what coaching is. They might have heard about it, but the majority of them have never experienced it. The bottom line is this: no matter which tool, strategy, method, or approach you use, you're in the business of solving problems. You can scream on top of your lungs that you are a coach, but no one will care unless you can solve a problem.

Keep this in mind as you read this book. Your success depends on it!

On What Level Do You Want to Play?

"I am on a mission, so I have to think big."
– Joel Christopher

Many coaches enter this field with a certain "baggage"– standards and rules they learned on their path to coming a coach. They put themselves in a "box," which limits their creativity and makes true business growth much more difficult.

Larina Kase, a business psychologist, marketing coach, and co-author of *The Successful Coach,* encourages coaches to think about what they *really* want when deciding upon what level they want to play. She says: "When I help coaching entrepreneurs to build their businesses, I always begin by asking them about their long-term business goals. The majority of coaches give me a very modest desirable income level. They base their goals on what they think they *can* do, not what they *want* to achieve. They consider what they've done so far and add a little to that number."

Hearing coaches express reserved visions has led me to question why coaches limit their goals. The answer, I believe, is that coaches limit their vision based on fear. The lack of assurance, nervousness, and fear of failure are common reactions for many entrepreneurs, not just coaches. We don't want to set the bar high and then fail.

We are all aware of the fact that there are TONS of coaches out there and that many are not financially successful and struggle to get clients and earn great income. As a result, coaches wonder whether they can be successful and are apprehensive to set their sites on a high-income level. Many coaches also limit their business goals due to a lack of confidence, feeling that until they achieve more, they cannot play on a bigger level.

While it is important to be realistic in setting your business goals, it's also important *not* to be limited by a lack of courage and confidence about whether you can make it. Be honest with yourself when deciding which level you WANT to play on. If you want it, you can achieve it. But if you limit your vision because you don't know whether you're capable of achieving it, you *will* limit your business profitability.

I tell my clients not to get caught up in the doom and gloom statistics. Coaching entrepreneurs are successful when they are proactive and dedicated to making their businesses take off. The lack of dedication and action is one explanation behind the statistics of low average incomes among so many coaches. If you are motivated, dedicated, and take consistent action, the chances are very good that you will be one of the people who achieves excellent income—if, of course, that's what you want.

Consider what level you want to play on and then push yourself to choose a higher level. Try it on for size, even if it feels uncomfortable. Know that if you commit to it, it will start to fit you very well. You'll shape your business to fit your vision."

Ramon Williamson, one of the most entrepreneurial and innovative thinkers I know, encourages coaches to get out of their "box" and think more creatively when it comes to building a business model.

Ramon believes that every coach has a different level of play. Some coaches just want to earn a part-time income. They want to coach every once in a while. Some coaches don't want to earn any money from coaching at all. It's just a volunteering thing for them. There are many different levels of play in the coaching world, so one of the most important things you can do to advance your goals is to find your level.

There are four *basic* levels of play that he talks about.

Number 1 is earning a part-time income from coaching, $5,000 to $30,000 annually or more.

Number 2 is enjoying an additional stream of income from coaching as part of your current business. Your primary business may be something else, but you want to integrate coaching into that business, earning $10,000 to $50,000 or more in annual income.

Number 3 is to enjoy full-time income from coaching. For the sake of illustration, I'm saying that's $60,000 or more a year.

Number 4 is to earn a six-figure income or better from coaching.

Wherever you want to play is okay. By identifying your level of play in coaching, however, you can better determine which strategies and models and mentors and resources you're going to utilize in your business and in your life.

Pick your level of play, then take action, build momentum, and make this your best coaching year ever!

Me, a Coach?

I know what you're probably thinking…

You haven't taken any coaching courses, attended a coaching school, or received a coaching certification. The truth is, you can still use the basic coaching models to help more of your clients succeed and add more revenue to your business.

If you have specialized expertise and don't offer coaching, you are leaving a lot of money on the table. Your customers, readers, students and members of your audience *want* to work with you. They need your guidance to help them get to the next level!

You can develop your own coaching programs, or team up with other coaches who'll work to support your customers. You can take your products or seminars and develop coaching programs around them. That's exactly what this book will teach you how to do, so let's dive right in!

How to Use This Book

Everyone reads books differently. I like to skim through the table of contents, flip through the pages then read a few paragraphs that catch my attention. I then go back and start reading, from the beginning.

While I hope that my journey touches and inspires you, simply reading this book alone will not result in the transformation you wish to experience. Allow me to suggest a few ways to use this book to advance and accelerate your success, like you never imagined possible!

The book is organized chronologically. By that I mean if you follow the steps in order, it'll make building your business a much easier and enjoyable process.

You may want to read this book from start to finish, underlining the important and profound discoveries you make, and the steps you want to implement. Usually, it drives me crazy when people write in books but if it helps you save time and get to the next level faster, I am giving you my sincere permission to write in *my* book!

You may also want to first skim through the book and read only the sections that apply to current situation. You may have already found a lucrative coaching niche, or created a product or two, and you feel like you need the next steps. In this case, go ahead and skip to the advanced sections, such as creating your coaching program, designing your "dream team," building recurring coaching income, and staying on the cutting edge of your industry.

When you discover something important, implement it right away! This happens to be one of my biggest success secrets – I act quickly on the new strategies I learn! If you're ready to keep an open mind and commit to your success, let's get started.

Part II
Getting Rich Is In the Niche

"The world is full of snail collectors…"

—Michael Koenigs

All Roads Lead to Niche

Some people will tell you that targeting a niche market will hurt your business. They say it may limit the type of clients you pursue, while limiting your income. They recommend not focusing on a specific niche, but letting the niche find you.

Others are convinced that no coaching business can succeed without a niche. The argument here is that consumers prefer to hire specialists, not generalists, to fix their problems. Unless you position yourself as an expert in a specific field, prospects may view you as a "jack of all trades, master of none."

On the other hand, choosing a niche doesn't mean choosing one forever. It simply means focusing on something you're best at, or have the greatest passion for, right now. You can always switch later but focusing on a niche is important at all times!

You will become effective only by becoming selective. In my estimate, 65% or more of struggling coaches haven't established a viable niche. They may *think* they have, but results speak louder than words.

So what's in a niche? A niche is simply a combination of a specialty and target audience.

My good friend David Frey, who is the creator of the Coaches Marketing Bootcamp, explains it with a brilliant and simple graph:

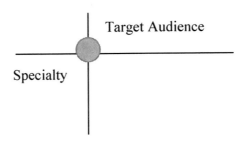

The horizontal line represents your specialty and the vertical line is your target audience. The intersection of these two lines creates a niche.

Many coaches have a specialty but no target audience–for example, the coach who specializes in communications, but targets everybody, including sales people, educators and medical practitioners. Others have a target audience, but don't offer a single core expertise. This is the coach who targets high-tech start-ups, but offers every service under the sun–from human resources consulting to product development and marketing.

If you have just one, but not the other, you may still enjoy some level of success. However, it's going to be much harder and take much longer to see results. I've seen perfectly great coaches struggle for years until they decided to do something about it!

It's not as difficult as you might think to pinpoint a winning niche. It may take some brainstorming and research but once you find it, sparks will fly! With a little luck and planning, you may find yourself tapping a rich vein of gold!

Here are some thought-provoking questions I like to ask my clients to help them narrow their search for a niche:

Questions to Help You Narrow Down a Niche

1. If you could do something all day long, what would it be?

2. If you were told to write a "how-to" book in a week, what subject would you choose?

3. If you had to write a series of 12 booklets, what topics would they include, and what would link them together?

4. What are some of your past career areas and interests?

5. What jobs do your friends and family members hold?

6. What obstacle(s) have you successfully overcome, and how?

7. Which of your life experiences could benefit others? Who, specifically, could benefit from them?

8. What is the biggest benefit clients would get from you?

Answering these questions will help narrow your list to three to five possibilities. And, once you identify your niche, half of your problems will be solved or–if you're a new coach–prevented.

Remember the niche formula I mentioned earlier?

Target Audience + Specialty = Niche

While this formula is still valid, let me put an important spin on it. This approach will really help you sharpen it:

Target Audience + Problem = Niche

In other words, choose a target audience, then find out what problem you can help them solve.

By the way, here is a quick crash course on terminology I've been using:

Target audience: the group of people you want to focus on reaching.

Specialty: what you help this group of people solve or achieve.

Niche: a combination of target audience and specialty.

What if you already have a coaching niche, but haven't achieved much success? Consider these three possible causes:

1) You're coaching part time or haven't truly committed to building your business. Let's face it, you can only be as successful as your level of commitment allows. If you have a full time job or a second business, that may hold you back from taking the steps that are essential to your success.

2) You've neglected one of the most important ingredients of a successful business–marketing and promotion. We will discuss specific marketing strategies for your business later in the book.

3) You've found your coaching niche, but not your "coaching habitat"–an ideal environment in which your business will grow and thrive. In other words, you may have a target audience and you may have a specialty but there is a missing link somewhere, a hidden gap that keeps you from growing your business. In the next section, I will help you identify any missing elements in your "coaching habitat" and accelerate your way to success.

Habitat is a combination of: all the elements in your specialty, target audience, and environment affecting the growth of your business and your lifestyle. Let's take a closer look at your own habitat in the next section.

The 8 Elements of a Successful Coaching "Habitat"

In the summer of 2000, I got kicked out of my internship, after being told I shouldn't be in computer science. "You could probably do well in information systems, management systems, or something else business-related," my boss told me.

Today, I can't thank him enough! Thank you, Gerry, for telling me I didn't belong in computer science. Eight hours of programming a day wasn't something I really wanted to do for the rest of my life–or even a couple of years. "I could trust you with my home, my money, my life, but I can't keep you working here. You're just not cut out for this," he said.

I wasn't.

At the time, I would have loved to prove him wrong, but luckily I was soon distracted by a new class called Internet Technology and became infatuated with building a web-based coaching business. *I found my "habitat!"*

(If I had persevered and continued my computer programming career, my whole life would have been one gigantic "yuck bucket!" as my friend and colleague, Sylva Leduc, calls it.)

A coaching "habitat" is an environment in which your business can grow and prosper. This habitat encompasses everything around you–people, technology, location, and lifestyle. Not every niche provides a suitable environment for your business. Pick the "wrong" habitat and your business will wither on the vine. The consequences of choosing the wrong coaching habitat may include:

-   Working with clients you don't like.

- Working with unsuitable partners–people with whom you can't find common ground.

- Lowered self-esteem and questioning your own credibility/abilities as a coach.

- Becoming saddled with a lifestyle you don't enjoy; trading wage slavery for enslavement to your own business.

Creating a coaching habitat is similar to creating a habitat for trees, vegetables and flowers. You need nutritious soil, ample water, enough sun, and space for growth. You'll also need to determine the best times to plant, and to identify existing vegetation and its likely effects on your "crop." At the risk of stretching the botanical analogy further, here are the eight basic ingredients needed for the ideal coaching habitat:

#1: Your Background (Soil). It will help you tremendously to be a member of your own target audience. By sharing a common background, it will be easier to develop a rapport and attract prospects. Targeting a niche with which you're personally familiar gives you added confidence and credibility as a coach–something many of your colleagues will lack.

#2: Specialized Interests (Defined Borders). Everyone belongs to a group–officially or mentally. For example, I belong to several different groups:

- Mothers
- Immigrants
- Self-employed, home-based business owners
- Internet business owners
- Home owners
- Small-town residents
- Computer users

What's more, within each group, members face similar challenges.

- **Mothers**: Raising children, juggling work and family.
- **Immigrants**: English probably being a second language, starting licensing or certification process from scratch.
- **Self-employed**: Managing home office, purchasing own medical insurance.
- **Internet business owners**: Generating consistent and predictable online sales.
- **Homeowners**: Doing taxes and maintenance, dealing with neighbors.
- **Small-town residents**: Having no high-quality theaters or concert halls, being physically isolated from centers of power and influence.
- **Computer users**: Don't get me started!

Members of your target audience have specialized interests and needs. They struggle with the same issues, and they are well aware of their struggles.

#3: Market Accessibility (Water). Do many of your prospects belong to particular associations? Do they read certain magazines or newsletters? You must be able to easily identify (and identify with) your prospects' concerns. If you had to list a dozen organizations and/or magazines used by your target market, could you do it? If not, reconsider your habitat.

#4: Growth Potential (Sun & Space). Your target market should be growing, not stagnating or dying. For growing markets, new products and services are developed every year. Events are organized, magazines are published, and so on. Research, read, and observe–this is the only way to stay on top of things within your target market.

#5: Coaching Issues (Food). When choosing a target market, be certain that there is a perceived need for your services.

Locate a target audience that faces a multitude of issues. If you work with female executives, helping them find a better job might be only *one* service you provide. You could also focus on time management, team building, conflict resolution, and other career-related issues your clients face after they land their "dream" job.

#6: Colleagues and Competitors (Existing Vegetation). When a multitude of coaches and other companies are selling their products to your target audience, it's a sign of a healthy market. If very few businesses are selling to these people, beware! There is probably a very good reason. When I perform market research, I look for "existing vegetation" before telling my clients, "IT'S A GREAT MARKET! GO FOR IT!"

#7: Marketing Strategies (Planting Time). What are the best methods for promoting your business? The effectiveness of print advertising, web sites, live events, teleseminars, direct mail, strategic alliances, and other tactics varies from market to market. Pricing is also a part of marketing strategy. What seems "cheap" in one market is shameless "gouging" in another.

A few years ago, I tried to put my music teaching and marketing experience together in a booklet, *77 Ways to Build Your Music Practice*. I priced it at $11.95, created a web site, and promoted the booklet on search engines. To my amazement, I received numerous e-mails from music teachers, sharing their stories and asking for advice.

"Buy my booklet!" I suggested. "It'll answer all your questions!"
"Oh, the price is too high," said several prospects.

Having previously worked with business owners who are accustomed to buying products online for $27 to $997, I was shocked. Obviously, music teachers had completely different price expectations! (Eventually, I lowered the price to $7.95 but I can't say this project was much of a success.)

Different audiences also possess different communication styles. Some time ago, I attended a teleseminar on buying residential properties. The host arrived five minutes late and the guest speaker didn't join us until halfway through the call. To my surprise, none of the participants hung up and nobody complained about the tardiness of the keynote speaker. I have no doubt that coaches would have been frustrated, annoyed, and even outraged by this situation.

The upshot: *know thine audience!* Study your market to learn how they think, attend events, read newsletters, and learn their language.

#8: Lifestyle and Habits (Traffic Patterns). Are you aligned with your prospects? Do you understand their lifestyles and goals? Are your values similar to theirs? Do you speak the same language? If not, you may find yourself "forcing" solutions on them, and getting little enjoyment from your work.

If you don't know how to locate prospects, then you haven't chosen a suitable target. Here's my personal list of criteria for selecting an ideal target audience:

Criteria For Selecting Ideal Target Audience

1. The group has specialized interests and needs.
2. They have a strong desire for what you offer.
3. You have (or you can create) a compelling reason for prospects to hire you instead of someone else.
4. You can easily reach individual prospects within the group.
5. The group is large enough to produce the volume of business you need.
6. The group is small enough for others to overlook it.
7. You are, or used to be, a member of this group.
8. Prospects can easily afford your products and services.
9. You enjoy working with people in this niche.

Many times observing other coaches who work in niche markets can help you spark an idea of your own. Below are some examples of coaches who successfully penetrated a new niche market.

Real-Life Examples of Coaching Niches

Ellen Ostrow, Ph.D.
http://www.LawyersLifeCoach.com

Having come from a psychotherapy background, Ellen first wanted to target professional women in mid-life. However, she soon realized that marketing to this group was very difficult because prospects didn't congregate in any specific place. So when a friend asked, "Who are your favorite clients in your clinical practice?" a light bulb appeared over her head. She'd been working with attorneys on many different levels, and had spent months researching what it's like to work in a law firm.

By creating topic-specific coaching groups and offering one-on-one coaching programs to attorneys worldwide, Ellen soon penetrated this lucrative niche market. Despite the fact that Ellen had no previous legal background, she is now the top coach for female attorneys.

Annie Meachem
http://www.fengshuimarketingcenter.com

In this example, feng shui became an ideal coaching habitat for a marketing expert. To create a profitable business around her expertise, Annie was looking for a target audience that was open to a particular spiritual concept and spoke the same language as her. She felt that she would really enjoy working with alternative professions and after doing some research, Annie found herself attracted to feng shui consultants. Prospects can be easily reached, the industry is growing, and its members are independent professionals seeking to build their businesses. In addition, this market appealed to Annie because of its members' alignment with the metaphysical idea of "energy."

But Annie was not a feng shui expert, so she needed a way to break into the market. By interviewing successful industry experts, she was able to create a marketing product for feng shui practitioners, receive insider information, and build the content for her new web site. Today, she runs the Feng Shui Marketing Center, which offers marketing assistance, coaching, and resources for feng shui consultants.

What Do Clients Really Want?

One of the mankind's secret desires is for someone to invent a mind-reading device. There are movies, books and anecdotes about it, but until such device is created, we have to use more traditional ways to "read the minds" of our clients.

The best thing about establishing a niche is that you can achieve a thorough grasp of how your clients think, how they may react to your offers, and what they want from you. It's easier to get inside the heads of a small, homogenous group than millions of potential clients. Still, you have to do your homework.

Start by immersing yourself in the target market for at least six months–total immersion. Lurk on relevant message boards to see what they're discussing, how they talk, what worries them, what annoys them, what's important to them. Attend live events, conferences, and trade shows. Take a look at how other companies communicate with your target audience. Get a feel for their writing style, the amount of detail they include, and their "hot button" issues.

Subscribe to relevant online newsletters and magazines, and read.

The whole purpose of defining your target audience is to know exactly what challenges these people face every day and what problems they've been trying to solve.

Before creating my first product for coaches, I spent six months participating in teleclasses designed for, and created by, coaches. I joined leading coaching organizations and signed up for a half-dozen coaching newsletters. I wanted to walk the walk and talk the talk! I wanted to feel what they feel, so I could understand their challenges.

By the way, you don't need to spend six months learning about your niche market. I watched as one of my fellow coaching entrepreneurs discovered, studied and dominated a niche market as the #1 coach within less than a month! It can be done, there is no question about it.

So, how do you develop products/services that your target audience really wants or needs? The answer is: survey, survey, survey–both before and after you roll out your offerings!

I work with many clients who wish to penetrate new niches. The first week's assignment is to locate five people to interview in person. During these interviews, a whole universe of issues becomes apparent. One client said, "Milana, I'm so glad I did this! I feel like I just took an enormous shortcut to business success! There is no way I would've gained this insider information if I hadn't done the interviews!"

After the initial interviews, survey your database at least once a year. Listen to your clients' concerns during your coaching sessions. You might unearth some hidden gems during these conversations!

For example, to prepare for writing this book, I surveyed 478 coaches in my database (you can see the results of this survey in *the back of the book*). The information and insights I gained from the survey results were essential to my understanding of what coaches deal with, what they worry about, and what solutions they need.

It's important to ask the right questions as you survey your database. Below is a list of questions you might want to ask.

23 Questions to Ask Your Target Audience

1. What kind of books or magazines do you buy?
2. What are your biggest challenges?
3. What keeps you up at night?
4. What would make your life absolutely perfect right now?
5. What accomplishments are you most proud of, in life or business?
6. What would you have done differently in life or business?
7. Where do you see yourself five years from now?
8. What recently discovered product or service really excites you?
9. What's your unique story? What makes you different from everyone else?
10. What do you desire most at this point in your life?
11. How do you prefer to receive training (books, teleclasses, in-person, etc.)?
12. What's your average monthly income?
13. What's your desired monthly income?
14. What are your top three monthly expenses?
15. What are the two most recent live events you attended?
16. What was the most expensive product or service you ever bought?
17. Which three web sites do you visit most frequently?
18. What do you look forward to every week? Every month?
19. If money weren't an issue, how could I best support you?
20. What are your top five priorities?
21. If you had to do it over again, what would you do exactly the same?
22. What are the top three things you'd like to accomplish in the next 6 months?
23. What's not working? What are you doing over and over again without the desired results?

Unrecognized Needs

It's important that your prospects already know they have a problem, and are willing to pay to solve it.

For example, if you coach independent restaurateurs, you may recognize that one of the main obstacles to profitability is poor service caused by high employee turnover. If the prospects don't agree that this is a problem, you will spend countless hours (and dollars) convincing them that you can help.

Your *ideal prospects* already know what they want and that's why they'll turn to you. Market your services based on recognized needs. Once you've acquired the client, *then* you can spend time educating him/her about the importance of solving unrecognized problems.

There are always exceptions to this rule, of course. A few years ago, I developed Assessment Generator. I didn't conduct any market research. Why? I developed the product to fulfill my *own* needs. I wanted to have a way to generate client leads automatically through online self-assessments and be able to pre-qualify my clients before taking them on. Today, hundreds of people use this tool to automate lead generation on their web sites.

The key was education: I wrote numerous articles about the value of lead generation, tracking client progress and creating surveys–everything for which the Assessment Generator can be used–and then offered my tool as a solution. It could have flopped. I could have wasted months of work. In this case, the people who read my articles came to understand their previously unrecognized need for this product. Now I see web site after web site that offers self-assessments!

Launching a major educational campaign is probably not the best use of time and resources if you're still in your start-up phase. Use common sense and intuition to decide if or when you should proceed in educating your audience and developing a solution.

Breaking New Ground

Have you ever heard the expression, "Pioneers get shot?"

Trying to "penetrate" a market or "habitat" that hasn't been defined or established is another somewhat "risky" strategy. It may take a lot of digging, pruning, cutting, and "rock removal" to create enough interest from a brand new group. In fact, if you're a new coach, I don't recommend trying to break new ground. There is usually a reason why a market hasn't been established and why nobody has "dared" create products or services for it.

- The group may be hard to reach.
- The group may have no purchasing power.
- The group may not be open to coaching or self-help.

I've always wanted to work with new immigrants trying to break into entrepreneurship and become successful in America. But deep in my heart–and from talking to my very own "focus group" (my family)–I knew they wouldn't be open to coaching.

It can be very expensive to penetrate a new market because it may require mass media advertising, trade shows, and costly research. Unless you're looking for a major challenge, stick with existing markets. Once you've established your coaching business and your "coaching habitat" is supporting you, you might consider expanding your frontiers.

Final Word on Niches and Specialties

You may be reading this and thinking, "I don't need to niche now—I can always do this later." I can't emphasize strongly enough how important it is to choose a niche and a "habitat" as soon as you start a business. Why waste valuable time when you can be building a long-lasting profitable business now?

If you are still struggling with this idea, let me share with you some of the biggest benefits of doing this. As soon as you make a decision to work inside a specific coaching niche, you'll be:

- Working with people you love every day.

- Creating strategic alliances that excite you.

- Treated like a celebrity at your industry conventions.

- Looking forward to every day in your office.

Part II: In a Nutshell

1. Choose your coaching niche as soon as you start your business - don't waste valuable time!

2. Determine what your expertise and specialty is, and what target audience would be willing to pay you to solve their problems. Go through the list of "habitat" elements and identify any issues you may need to explore further or adjust to.

3. Study your niche to find out what some of the biggest challenges your target audience experiences, what solutions are already being offered to them, and how you can reach them easily.

Part III
Pick Your Coaching Model

"I don't want to do business with those who don't make a profit, because they can't give the best service."
—Richard Bach

What Kind of Coach Are You?

A "gazillion" ideas and opportunities are thrown at you every time you open your email or attend an event. Unfortunately, this can overwhelm, frustrate, and even paralyze you–it's difficult to be sure which direction is best.

What I am about to share with you will change all that. Regardless of which path you want to take as a coach, understanding this concept will get you there ten times faster. It will allow you to focus and accelerate your growth. Everything you do will build on what you've already done before, so the growth will be exponential.

Let me ask you a question: What kind of business do you want to build? As a coaching entrepreneur, you can travel or stay at home, visit companies or run large conference calls, organize live events or write books, run coaching groups or speak on your own talk show.

The choice is yours, but how do you know what's the right choice for *you*?

I've met many coaches who spent years building a full practice only to discover that they dread working with clients one-on-one. I've also met coaches who built an international coaching business traveling around the world, and now can't wait to quit the "gypsy" lifestyle to work from home.

Wouldn't it be great to create a business you truly enjoy today and will enjoy for years to come? How can you design a business model that builds on your strengths, passions and goals?

Coaching business model—that's the concept that virtually no one thinks about when starting a business. Simply put, a coaching business model is where the money comes from in your business; in other words, it's your source of revenue. Ideally, it's where you also have the most fun!

When thinking about your business model, you need to consider your unique personality, coaching style, goals and lifestyle preferences. You probably don't want to end up going on a week-long business trip every month if your goal is to home-school your children.

I would be miserable if I had to take a lot of out-of-state trips or coach my clients early in the morning (I like to sleep in), so I built my business in such a way that I don't have to. It's not just about my schedule—it's about choosing a business model that allows me to use only the strategies that suit my life.

Later in the book I will share with you the specific strategies and programs you can incorporate into your business model. But first, let me reveal to you the top five most commonly used coaching business models.

As you read about each model, keep in mind that you can mix and match. You can combine multiple models, although one model will always dominate your business, based on your preferences, goals and personality.

1 Individual Coaching Model

This is the most common model, also considered "traditional" coaching. Most new coaches start out with this model, adding more leverage to their business later. If this is your predominant business model, then you probably do a lot of one-on-one coaching. You are *Practitioner*.

There is a high risk of burnout because individual coaching can be quite intense and energy-consuming, depending on your style. Just be aware of this and try to diversify your business by combining it with other coaching models.

2 Group Coaching Model

One of the best ways to leverage your time and increase the number of people you reach is to coach groups of people. It is also a great way to have a lot of fun in your business! If this is your predominant model, then you do you most of your coaching by working with groups. You probably run multiple coaching groups, enjoying the energy and dynamics of a group environment.

I've seen two variations of the group coaching model: ongoing and time-defined. The ongoing groups can last for many years, and new members can join at any time. The time-defined groups have a beginning and an end, which means that you need to fill your groups every time you start a new one.

Group Coaching Model is very similar to Individual Coaching Model in that you still have to do a lot of coaching personally. If you love the coaching process but want to keep your business growing and leverage your time better, this may be an ideal model for you.

3 Training Coaching Model

If you get energized by a large group of people and enjoy traveling, consider the Training Coaching Model. You will do most of your coaching "on stage," inspiring and motivating your audience to take action. You can offer coaching groups to those participants who would like implementation support, and even one-on-one coaching to individuals who are looking for high-level support. Such high profile coaches as Anthony Robbins, Rhonda Britten, Marcia Wieder, and Harv Eker all use this model. They also have a team of other coaches who work with their attendees.

4 Membership Coaching Model

The Membership-based Coaching Model is probably one of the most lucrative financial models you can ever create in your business. It allows you to grow exponentially and enjoy consistent residual income every month. Coaching clubs, inner circles, and mastermind groups are all examples of membership-based coaching models.

Although you can incorporate group coaching and training into this model, it allows you to deliver value in other ways besides coaching. You can invite and interview guest experts, have a members-only forum on your web site, create special events for your members, and offer helpful resources inside the member area.

This model is much more flexible than other business models and gives you plenty of free time in your life. If you are highly entrepreneurial and get excited by new opportunities and ideas, this is probably the best model for you.

5   Info-Product Coaching Model

If you are an expert on a certain subject, and love doing research, writing and creating information products, then this model will give you plenty of time to enjoy yourself. If you use this model in your business, chances are you don't mind having little contact with your customers, spending most of your time in your home office creating new products. You are probably a prolific writer, always full of ideas, and can develop dozens of ebooks, CDs, home-study manuals, and audio products in a short period of time.

To increase your revenue beyond just products, you can offer short-term coaching or consulting to your customers. Obviously, as you build your customer database, you can hold occasional training events and develop high-ticket products over time.

As you look at these five business models, here are some questions to ask yourself:

-   What's my current predominant coaching model?

-   Where does 51 or more percent of my income come from?

-   Which model appeals to me the most?

Picking the right coaching model is essential to your level of success, your personal satisfaction and your lifestyle.

When I start working with my clients, the first step is to determine what their ideal business model is. We go through a series of questions and statements to identify what their business should look like, and which elements should never be a part of their business.

Another great way to determine what your business model should be is to take a personal analysis assessment, such as DISC or Myers Briggs. You will understand what types of activities require high energy level from you, and which activities come natural. An assessment will tell you about your ideal work environment and your strongest personal talents. With results "staring" you in the face, it's easy to pick the right model!

Developing Your Building Blocks

Regardless of what business model you choose and how your business will look, one thing is essential for you to develop—your building blocks. Let's take a look at what this means, why it's important and how you can create your own building blocks.

Building blocks are the core principles and beliefs you bring to your clients. They are your primary teaching points. Together they represent your core process, your "program." Once you determine what your building blocks are, you can build your entire business around them.

Before you identify your building blocks, you need to be clear about your core message. Answer these questions: What is your message to your target audience? What is the number one problem you're trying to solve? What are you *really* saying?

What *I* am really saying is that in order to be truly successful as a coach you need to become an entrepreneur and a leading expert in your niche—this is my core message. To make this happen, you first need to choose a niche, then decide on your ideal coaching model, build a market presence, create passive and residual income sources, develop a self-propelled business, and finally, become a "mover and shaker" in your industry.

These six steps are my building blocks. They are a part of everything I "teach and preach." All my coaching programs and products have been developed around these building blocks. In fact, this book is based on the same six essential elements, and so is my ultimate business system.

Student Success Systems were created by Sonja Martin, former school principal and education consultant. Her core message is that parents, teachers and students can work together to achieve extraordinary student success. In the heart of her systems are these five essential components she developed and strongly believes in[1]:

1. <u>Effective Parent Partnerships</u> which empower parents to assist their children's learning.

2. <u>High Leverage Motivation Techniques</u> to assure optimum learning efforts from every child, every day.

3. <u>Alignment of standards,</u> benchmarks, report cards, assessments and instruction.

4. <u>Focused Instruction</u> based on the learning needs of every child.

5. <u>Individual Student Data</u> that is easily read and understood by teachers, parents and students.

From these five building blocks, Sonja Martin developed achievement guides for teachers, parents and home-school families. She delivers her message at conferences and workshops around the country.

Here's another quick example. If you were a coach to new landlords, your core message could be this: you can become a wealthy landlord without sacrificing your lifestyle. The five building blocks you would teach to your clients might be finding good property, getting quality tenants, choosing a solid property manager, learning to make money with rentals, and studying the landlord-tenant law. All your articles, seminars, programs and home-study courses would deliver your core message through teaching these five elements.

If your target market are people who run employment agencies, business relationships may be an important area you coach

---

[1] Quoted from Sonja Martin's web site at <u>www.studentsuccesssystems.com</u>

them in. But what's your position on business relationships? Perhaps, you believe that every employment agency must position themselves as a problem solver to be successful. This concept can be taught and implemented through a series of action steps.

What's a Building Block?

Each building block is a teachable concept that can be implemented through a series of action steps or mental shifts. It is not just an area you want to discuss, but rather a key success ingredient that contains your opinion about something.

As Donald Trump said to Donny Deutsch on *The Big Idea* TV show, there is no middle ground. You either like me or you don't (in which case you side with Rosie O'Donnell).

In other words, you must have a strong position on anything you coach or teach. When you take middle ground, you lose your edge.

Identifying your own core message and your building blocks is the number one secret to end feeling overwhelmed once and for all. It also allows you to take a stand and experience a great level of confidence as a coach. My clients are usually amazed at how much clarity this brings into their business. They can't believe they've been operating without their building blocks in place for months or even years!

Once you know what your message is and how you can help people accomplish their goals, you can quickly start developing your products, workshops, training events, and group coaching programs!

Choosing the Perfect Coaching Program Model

Originally, my business was a web design and Internet consulting firm. I conducted occasional coaching sessions with clients who needed "handholding," but I hadn't given my services any structure. In November 2002, I offered a teleclass and although I'd conducted teleclasses before, I was extremely excited about this one. All of the material was original and based on my own research findings.

When the class was over, a couple of people asked if I offered coaching on the topics we'd discussed during the call, and whether I could send them information about my coaching services. I didn't have anything to send, but didn't want to miss out on new business. So I quickly put together a 12-week program, briefly outlined the topic for each week, gave it a title, and sent it to every Teleclass participant.

Those who'd inquired about my coaching services instantly signed up for this program. Over the next few weeks, whenever people asked how I could help them, I sent the same file. Within a few weeks, I enrolled seven new coaching clients–all as a result of creating this coaching program. It was a truly eye-opening experience! Here's what it made me realize:

-   The term "coaching services" is extremely vague. People new to the concept won't know what to expect, unless you *specify* the result clients will get and the benefits they'll gain by working with you.

-   Prospects may be hesitant in committing to ongoing coaching–coaching that may go on forever, like Freudian psychoanalysis. They may be more comfortable with a program limited to a certain number of sessions or weeks.

- It's much easier to define specific benefits and results if you know which issues you'll work on with the client.

In other words, creating a coaching program is a must! Based on my research, most coaches don't use the word "program" on their web sites–they simply refer to their services as "coaching." Even those who use the term "coaching program" use it incorrectly. Most of the time, they simply mention the fact that they offer a program but don't provide any specific details.

A coaching program must have a name, a defined time limit, and specific goals that clients will achieve by the program's end!

People are attracted to specific programs rather than just coaching, because they can easily understand what to expect from a coaching program. They can see a tangible result, which is what every client wants.

In the next few pages, I will show you how you can:

- Choose the right coaching program model that works for your business and your lifestyle.

- Put your program together from your existing knowledge, experience, and materials.

- Make your program extremely valuable so it's irresistible to your target clients.

- Develop a pricing strategy that appeals to customers and is very lucrative for you.

I will also give you some of my very best tips to manage your clients, create the lifestyle you really want, and avoid burn-out by creating balance in your business.

There are probably as many program models as there are creative coaches in the world. Some coaching models, however, have become widely popular, thanks to their consistent success. Each program type fits a different coaching style and business model, so be sure to check out all of the models here before making a choice.

Model #1: Introductory Coaching Program

One popular model is the "introduction to coaching." This allows new clients to get a taste of your coaching style and experience the impact of coaching on their lives. The program's duration can vary from 4 to 12 weeks, but you'll probably need to schedule at least six sessions to impact your client's life or business. The goal of this program is to demonstrate what coaching can do, and it can be used as an effective alternative to a complimentary session.

This program model may not allow clients to experience the true impact of long-term coaching. In addition, an introductory program may attract people who will never commit to a long-term relationship.

On the other hand, it's simple to put together and allows you more time to decide if a client will be a good fit in the long term. For example, to enroll clients in a 12-month *Happy Relationship for Life* program, you might offer a four-week introductory program called *Six Principles of Healthy Relationships*. You'd introduce the same concepts in both programs, but wouldn't delve as deep during the introductory program. When the four-week program is completed, you invite qualified participants to enroll into your longer coaching program.

Model #2: Action Plan Coaching Program

An Action Plan Coaching Program is designed to accomplish a specific goal within a relatively short time period. This program is always laser-focused and promises a very tangible result. The model is best used for business coaching and usually includes some form of training or consulting.

Any "how-to" article can be turned into an action-plan coaching program. For example, an article entitled *How to Put Together an Effective Speaking Presentation* could be converted into a six-week program called *The Perfect Public Seminar*. An article entitled *How to Write and Publish Your Own e-Book* can be turned into a seven-week *Publish Your Own E-Book* program. That's exactly what I did!

This program is my favorite one. I find it easy to leverage my time by writing a "how-to" article, which I send to thousands of my subscribers, which I then turn into a coaching program for those who need more guidance.

I also find it extremely rewarding to take clients from point "A" to point "B" in such a short period, giving them the skills and knowledge needed for future projects. And if the client isn't a good fit or less than pleasant to work with, it's easy to discontinue the relationship.

Based on a "how-to" concept, an action-plan coaching program is also simple to create. And since it focuses on a specific task and can be easily explained to prospects, it's also easier to market than other programs. This model is as close as it gets to a tangible product, such as a book or taped seminar, and products are always easier to sell than services.

A word of caution here: When a client completes this program, he or she may not need your services again, limiting your coaching relationship to the length of the program. It's also very easy to fall victim to "project scope creep," providing more and more services to your clients without receiving extra compensation. For example, e-book publishing can get very technical. If a client isn't computer savvy and gets frustrated, I may end up doing some of the work for him. A speaking coach may end up editing her client's presentation and a sales coach might be asked to edit her client's sales script. Anticipate the extra time you'll need to help such clients and price your program accordingly.

Both, #1 and #2 program types can be used with Individual and Group Coaching models.

Model #3: Coaching Gym

The idea of The Coaching Gym originated with Dan Sullivan's *Strategic Coach* system, which included quarterly workshops for clients and an unusual, but effective, weekly work schedule. Thanks to Chris Barrow, a British business coach who started using this system and teaching others, this model is now used by hundreds of coaches worldwide. Besides offering the potential for building a million-dollar coaching practice, this model also promises an exciting and rewarding lifestyle.

The "gym" is just one method in which coaching is delivered in this model. It includes access to the coach by e-mail or telephone three days a week during specified hours. Any time a client needs to speak to a coach, he or she can call for a 15-minute laser-coaching session. Although access to the coach is unlimited and clients can call or e-mail every day, experience shows that only 20% of your clients will actually take advantage of this access.

The "gym" can also be combined with:

- Live quarterly workshops
- Workbooks, assessments, and web site resources
- 1-2 telephone group conferences a month
- A weekly workout log

The weekly workout log is just an e-mail reminder to visit the web site's client area to answer questions about accomplishments and challenges of the week. "Not every client responds, but it does create auto-accountability and demonstrates that we care every week," says Chris.

The Coaching Gym is the system that allowed Chris Barrow to evolve beyond one-on-one coaching calls (which many coaches dread). It also enabled him to work with many more clients than individual coaching would allow, bringing his practice to the million-dollar level. Other benefits of the model include:

- Enjoying 12 weeks of vacation spread throughout each year.
- Coaching clients three full days per week and having three-day weekends.
- Focusing one full day every working week on practice building.

The Coaching Gym model is not for everyone. As a mother of two young children, I decided not to implement the program. Being in a "telephone standby" mode–even for just three days a week–and traveling four times a year would be too stressful. This program also generates sizeable overhead, which includes contractors and freelancers, travel expenses, and workshop-related accommodations.

There is a very clear marketing strategy used to promote this type of program–a free newsletter that invites participation in the free teleclass that promotes the live event that introduces the main coaching program. This is done year round, with a focus on starting the program in January, and conducting the events in the fall. "I love the idea of only having to recruit new clients once a year. This keeps my cash flow stable, and means that I can focus my peak marketing for the fall," says Chris.

Since there is no traditional one-on-one coaching involved, it's realistic to take on many more clients than you're accustomed to working with. At $5,400 a year per client (approximately $450 a month), enrolling 185 clients a year will create a million-dollar coaching business.

Don't worry about being overwhelmed by the workload generated by 185 clients. As a rule, only 20% of clients will take *full advantage* of the coaching gym, calling for 15-minute coaching sessions, or emailing with questions every week. The other 80% will be content with the other ways you deliver coaching. They know you're there!

The Coaching Gym program combines the elements of Individual and Group Coaching models, as well as Training model.

Model #4: Mastermind Group Coaching

The concept of the Mastermind group was introduced by Napoleon Hill almost a hundred years ago, in his best-selling book *Think and Grow Rich*.

"No two minds ever come together without thereby creating a third, invisible intangible force, which may be likened to a third mind," he wrote.

The two most popular types of Mastermind groups are *industry-specific* and *peer-based*. Industry-specific involves professionals who represent the same industry: health care, real estate, executive coaching, management consulting, etc. However, people in the same industry may be hesitant to join a Mastermind group for fear of releasing valuable ideas to the competition.

Industry-specific groups are most effective when participants can't compete with one another–for example, accounting firm owners who live and work in different cities, states, or even countries.

Peer-based mastermind groups involve people at the same professional level. Participants could include executives from diverse, non-competing industries–for example, CEOs of insurance, pharmaceutical, and financial companies.

The format of a mastermind group is only limited by the leader's imagination! I like to structure it in a very simple way. "What are you most excited about this month?" and "What is your challenge today so we can help you?" are the two questions I ask my members.

Mastermind Your Way to Success!

The very first mastermind group I created consisted of three people–three businesswomen working from home.

One of the women who joined the group conducted her business right out of her bedroom. While working on creating her products and attracting clients, she was also managing her husband's business and being constantly interrupted by her young son. Her biggest concern was that her family was not taking her business seriously and that was extremely discouraging to her.

Fast forward three years later... She now has her own office in a renovated basement of their house; She hired an assistant who helps her take care of her business and her son. And, she convinced her husband to hire his own assistant, who helps him manage his clients and his schedule.

This amazing transformation wouldn't have been possible without the support, inspiration, and the strategies born during our monthly mastermind group meetings.

Participants in a mastermind group leave each session re-energized, full of ideas and new possibilities, and highly committed. Something amazing happens when you are in a group of other like-minded people who are working toward similar goals.

The size of the group can vary from 3 to 100 people. I can see the jaws of some experienced mastermind group leaders drop right now, but let me tell you something: With a large number of people in a mastermind group, everyone benefits by listening, observing, taking notes, brainstorming new ideas, even if they don't get to talk each time.

One of the biggest benefits of joining a mastermind group is receiving valuable feedback about product ideas or business situations from other members. When you have several people brainstorming a project, incredible breakthroughs happen. Mastermind group coaching allows people to reach a level of accomplishment they could never achieve on their own.

The great thing about this model from the business perspective is that you can launch several mastermind groups, focused on different topics and geared toward different audiences. There is no agenda to prepare–just come ready to share your successes and challenges, and help other members.

The value of your mastermind group depends on the value each participant can bring. Screen members to ensure they're a good fit for the group or you risk compromising the overall value.

While this is a great model for those who thrive on teamwork and brainstorming, participants may still require individual attention from the coach. Take this into account when pricing your program and expect to be contacted by some clients.

The mastermind element can be a part of any business model, although you'll see it used most frequently in Group Coaching and Membership Coaching models.

Model #5: Training and Certification Program

A certification program works well with a very specific target audience whose objective is to improve their skills and become certified for credibility. To deliver a program in this format, a coach must be highly qualified and experienced in the area of certification. The difference between this model and the others is that it's usually a business-to-business program. Each certification program is designed for professionals.

The simplest way to deliver a certification-coaching program is by offering weekly telephone sessions that follow a curriculum, with individual e-mail support between calls. Some programs include a membership web site with a discussion forum, resources, and a newsletter as a value-added benefit. There should also be certain certification requirements, which may include an exam, teaching ethical standards–anything needed to maintain your program's credibility.

Your program may also include training materials such as audios, books, and manuals, as well as an automatically delivered e-course with assignments, exercises, and self-tests.

Because of their high-perceived value, certification programs are usually priced higher than standard coaching programs. For example, the Guerilla Marketing Coach certification program, which includes 12 weeks of training, 12 audios and a 180-page manual, is priced at $1,895 (or $632 a month) per participant. Less recognized programs can be priced lower, but by including more value-added benefits (e.g., manuals, audios, assessments, e-mail support, etc.), you can increase the price accordingly.

Program requirements must be strictly enforced for the certification to have any kind of effect and credibility. Preferably, your program must become a recognized standard of certification among other professionals and potential clients. In other words, you must create and maintain a strong brand recognition by asking (or even requiring) that your graduates post the program's certification logo on their web sites and other marketing materials, promoting it in trade publications, giving interviews about your program, and holding live conferences or tele-conferences.

You may also develop a referral system for your graduates and offer post-graduation support to add more value to your package.

In addition to attractive revenue potential and the satisfaction you get from helping others, you will also enjoy a great deal of credibility from being a certification program's founder and leader. You can leverage this credibility when looking for speaking engagements and coaching clients, or if you ever decide to send a book proposal to the editors of a publishing company.

You may also continue growing your "school" by developing new coaching programs and courses, adding more value and more options for students. You can also earn additional revenue by up-selling products and announcing events in an ongoing newsletter for all past and current participants.

This program type can be used by coaches who are leaning toward Group, Membership and Training Coaching models.

Model #6: Inner Circle Model

The Inner Circle format is great for your high-level coaching clients, whom you'll charge a monthly, quarterly or annual fee. Some coaches refer to this type of program as a "coaching club" or "private membership," and provide additional resources in an online, password-protected member area. The words "inner circle" imply that members are selected based on a specific criteria and are considered an "elite" group.

Regardless of what you call it, the main distinction between an inner circle and other coaching programs is what it revolves around–a highly successful person with near-celebrity status whose clients are actually fans. You don't have to be a celebrity to start an inner circle, but you'll need some first-hand experiences and achievements to share with the group.

I started "Milana's Inner Circle" because it suited my blunt and to-the-point laser-coaching style and my desire to work only with highly self-motivated members. I chose not to accept any part-timers, because their level of commitment and innovation is usually limited by their "part-time" mentality.

My members are looking for practical and candid advice, even if it completely contradicts what they learned, heard, or read before. They know that my knowledge comes from first-hand experience and years of testing, and are willing to implement the strategies I share with them.

I love the Inner Circle format because it allows me to deliver huge value in a short period of time. A few hours a month of training and mastermind calls create incredible breakthroughs and strategies that members are able to implement as soon as they're off the phone.

I learned something else about myself while running the Inner Circle. I become incredibly passionate and generous when I know that my work helps my members solve problems. That's why I frequently develop new programs and products, and let my members have them for no extra charge. I get to create new products, add value to my Inner Circle members, and generate revenue by selling them to non-members. That's the model I use in my business.

Bringing It All Together: The "Coaching Diamond"

Choosing the right model is essential for your success. It has to fit your lifestyle, your personality, your short and long-term financial goals, and how you want your business to look three years from now.

Most coaches build their business in "pieces," creating random products and programs that don't really build on each other.

What I am about to show you will help you bring all the pieces together. Developing your own Coaching Diamond™ will allow you to quickly find a place for each of your products and programs. You will also be able to tell if there are any "gaps" you need to fill, and create maximum financial rewards with your business model.

Some people call me the "product queen." That's because over the years of running my business, I developed dozens of products, programs, services, and events for my clients. In fact, my predominant business model was Info Products model.

While it's exciting to bring a new product to my target audience, I always used to feel like I was creating just *another* product. There was no system to my approach. I created products and programs as the ideas came to me.

Then, I was introduced to the concept of a "product funnel." You've seen it—it's a cone-shaped figure, where each tier represents a different program or level of access to you. Here's an example you've probably seen before:

Product Funnel

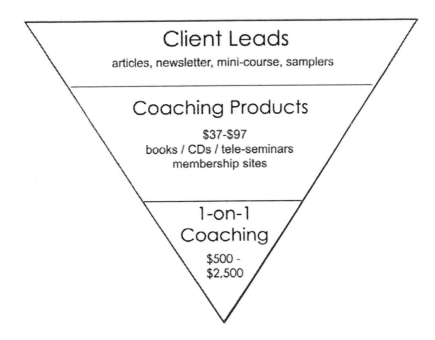

Each tier is more expensive than the previous one and the ultimate goal is to "funnel" a prospect from becoming a lead to enrolling as a coaching client.

As I "filled" my funnel with products and services, I saw two problems:

1. Since I could only work with half a dozen coaching clients at a time, I would have to say "no" to everyone else who needed my support. So no matter how hard I worked to get clients, I would have to turn most of them away.

2. My products solved problems and educated my customers about important topics. What I didn't have in

place was an all-in-one system where I could teach my overall process.

So, I needed to find a way to support more clients without sacrificing my lifestyle. I also needed to package the step-by-step process I use with my clients.

That's when the light bulb went on! A product funnel works great for any other business but in coaching, there needs to be another level—implementation support.

Take a look at the picture on the next page. The Coaching Diamond™ starts out just like a product funnel: you need to generate leads and convert them into buyers by selling your products.

Then, instead of offering one-on-one coaching, you offer a *coaching system*—your step-by-step process packaged as a live event, a set of audio CDs, or an accelerated group-coaching program.

Coaching Diamond™ Model

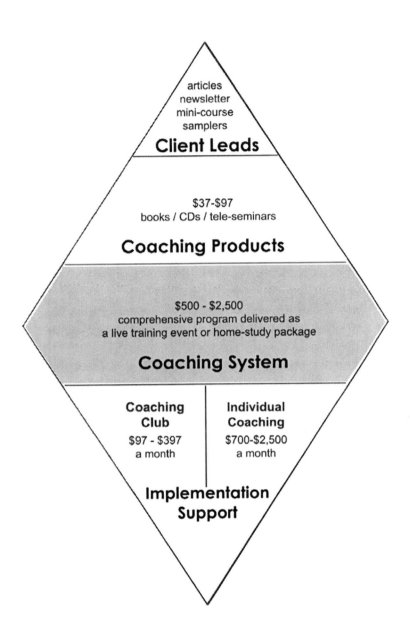

articles
newsletter
mini-course
samplers
Client Leads

$37-$97
books / CDs / tele-seminars
Coaching Products

$500 - $2,500
comprehensive program delivered as
a live training event or home-study package
Coaching System

Coaching Club | **Individual Coaching**
$97 - $397 a month | $700-$2,500 a month

Implementation Support

Your coaching system will teach your clients the process for achieving their goal. Once they understand the process and are ready to implement the steps, they will require additional support from you. You can offer support through a coaching "club" or individual coaching.

By using this business model you'll be able to accomplish three important things:

1. You can work with a limited number of individual coaching clients, while charging higher fees for one-on-one access to you.

2. You will build residual income source into your business, which is absolutely essential for generating six to seven figures in coaching.

3. You will feel good about being able to offer coaching to those who cannot afford to work with you one-on-one!

4. Having a system will create the need for your coaching.

To demonstrate how the "Coaching Diamond" model works in real life, I'll use my own business as an example.

"Coaching Diamond" in Action

Every "Diamond" model will look slightly different, depending on the products and services you offer, and the lifestyle preferences you have. For example, if you enjoy traveling and meeting clients in person, you may want to deliver your "coaching system" as a live event. I prefer working out of my home office and doing as little travel as possible. That's why I packaged my system into a home-study course on audio CDs.

Let's take a look at how my diamond looks:

Milana's "Coaching Diamond"

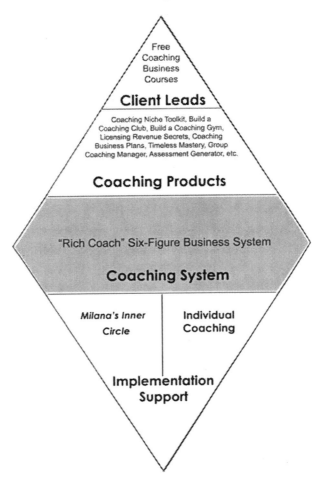

At the top of the diamond are my free coaching business courses. Each course is automatically delivered via e-mail to anyone who requests it from my web site.

On the next level you'll see the various products I offer in practice building, practice management, and passive income areas. Each product teaches a specific strategy or offers a tool for automating or simplifying a daunting task.

In the center of the diamond is my *Coaching Millions Lifestyle Business Building System*. It is based on the step-by-step process I used to reach a high income level, become one of the leading experts in my industry, and create a lifestyle I have always wanted. It is the same process I teach to my private clients, and it's packaged into a set of audio CDs for convenience.

Anyone who is looking for further support, coaching, and ideas can either enroll into Milana's Inner Circle coaching club, or work with me on an individual level.

If a prospect has ever said to you, "I can't afford coaching right now," start a coaching club! If they truly want to work with you, this will be the best way for them to get coaching without paying high monthly fees. With your help and the help of other coaching club members, they'll be ready to hire you at the next level!

Making Your Coaching Program Irresistible

Once you choose a program model, it's time to start assembling your package. The easiest way to develop content for your program is to document a process for achieving a specific result.

For example, if you're creating a coaching program for people who want to negotiate a higher salary, the process might consist of three steps:

1. Planning–what needs to happen before the negotiation begins: evaluating job performance, communicating with managers, learning special skills, etc.

2. Preparation–documents, checklists and tools necessary to create a negotiation strategy, etc.

3. Approach–how to get started, how to handle objections, what to do if negotiations don't go well, etc.

If you're creating a short-term program, think about giving it a catchy name. Here are some examples:

- Happily Ever After: a 16-Week Program for New Couples.

- The Golden Years: an 8-Week Program for the Newly Retired.

- Effective Manager: a 6-Week Program for Brand New Managers.

- A Second Chance: a 12-Week Program for Re-married Couples.

If you've ever delivered a workshop or written an article, you already have a coaching program in you.

Regardless of what model you choose or how long it runs, you need to make your program irresistible. In other words, it needs to have high-perceived value to potential clients.

Have you ever purchased something just because you wanted a bonus that came with it? I have! A powerful bonus not only adds value, but also makes your coaching program easier to sell. In addition, a good bonus enhances the actual content of the program.

I have a question I always ask myself to create a valuable offer. This question is absolutely "magic!" It helps me come up with a great bonus my prospects will rush to get. Here is the question: *"What would be worth a thousand dollars to my clients right now?"*

Consider the earlier example–negotiating a higher salary. Let's give this program a title: "3 Steps to Successful Salary Negotiation." What could you include as a bonus to make this program 10 times more valuable to the client? How about three audio demonstrations of actual salary negotiations? It might be tough to get real-life recordings, but you can easily use role-play or simulated examples by recording them with a client or a colleague. Another great bonus might be copies of actual query letters that resulted in salary increases. Who wouldn't want a proven model for getting more money out of their boss?

The point is, your offer must be irresistible. How you price it is a huge part of how people perceive your program, so let's talk about it next.

Developing a Powerful Pricing Strategy

One of the biggest reasons so many coaches are struggling financially and in their work-life balance is pricing.

Years ago, I was sitting in a crowded hotel conference room as Dave Buck, the CEO of Coachville, led a seminar. Had you entered the room around 11:30 that morning, you would have heard everyone reciting the following: "I charge $500 a month. I charge $500 a month. I charge $500 a month." This felt strange and uncomfortable because most attendees charged far less.

The participants who already charged $500 or more a month knew something I didn't. Setting your coaching fees is not just about the pricing. It's about your overall business strategy and your relationship with money.

In the next section, my goal is not only to show you how to develop an effective pricing strategy and earn what deserve, but also to change the way you think about your time and the value you bring to your coaching clients.

How much should you charge clients? Or better yet, how do you convince prospects to sign up regardless of how much you're charging?

When most coaches decide how much to charge, they usually pick a figure with which they feel comfortable, often under-pricing their services. This is the most ineffective method for setting a coaching fee.

In the next few minutes, I will share with you some of my biggest discoveries, lessons, and observations about developing a pricing strategy. Take these tips to heart—I've tested them hundreds of times, and they work!

Enhancing Your Credibility

Most people judge the quality of a product or service by its price. You can just as easily lose a sale by charging too little rather than charging too much. Rightly or wrongly, clients often judge your credibility by your fee structure.

If you were searching for a business coach, and found someone charging just $250 a month, what would be your first reaction? Mine would be, "She's probably a newbie who is still learning how to coach."

Then consider the business coach who charges $950 a month. Most people would immediately think, "She must have worked in her field for years!" or "She must be really good!" or "Her practice is probably full. I'll be lucky to get her!"

Many organizations won't hire a coach who charges less than $1,000 to $5,000 a month. I'm not suggesting that you should wake up one day and say: "Hmm ... I've already coached five clients. I'll double my rates and see what happens." Certain things need to be in place before you can do this successfully:

- You must specialize, offering something other coaches can't, won't, or don't.

- You must have achieved a certain level of success with previous clients, so you feel confident in your abilities and can offer client testimonials.

- You must have tools or systems in place that offer a proven "formula" for success.

Attracting "Serious" Clients

As a rule, the more the client pays, the more committed to success he is, the harder he works toward his goals, the happier he is with your coaching, and the more fulfilled you are as a coach. That's why I don't believe in offering discount fees for coaching services. If someone can't afford to hire you, either suggest group coaching or sell him or her a product.

Some might argue: "But if I agree to work with a coaching client at a discount, she might refer other people to me. The value of this client may double or triple in the long run!" Maybe that's true. But what kind of referrals will you get? Chances are you'll end up with more and more "discount" clients ... not the best scenario since you'll simply work harder for very little money.

Instead of accepting a "discount" client, consider using that time more efficiently, adding leverage and growing your business assets:

- Create a coaching group

- Write a book

- Give a workshop

- Publish a newsletter

- Strategize and plan

- Connect with a joint venture partner

When you agree to cut your fees, you don't just sacrifice money. You sacrifice your valuable time–time that could be spent marketing to prospects who are willing to pay high fees.

I would make an exception to this "no discounts" rule only if these three things were true:

- I believe the client has great potential and is highly self-motivated so I wouldn't have to put in a lot of energy convincing her that something works.

- The coaching period is slated to last for a short, well-defined period (no longer than 90 days), and will never be offered to that client again.

- I could record the sessions and use them as a case study, as part of a product, or in my work with other clients. (Of course, I would keep the client's name and other sensitive information confidential.)

In the cases above, I wouldn't even think of this person as a client. I'd think of her as a protégé–a "Mozart in the making" for whom I'm willing to lower my standard fees.

Perceived Value

Pricing is a great indicator of your confidence level. It's the value you decide to put on your time and expertise. Once, I bought an hour of someone's time for $350 just to pick his brain. What's an hour of your time is worth to a client?

In other fields, there are traditional ways to find the price that's "just right," but in coaching it's quite different. Most coaches will price themselves at the level other coaches do in similar fields. They'll look at the average coaching fees ($145 an hour for business coaches, $95 for life coaches) to find their price points. Finally, many coaches price their services at whatever they feel comfortable with.

In reality, you'll find coaches who charge $45 an hour and you'll find coaches who charge $500 an hour. It all depends on the value they can deliver to their clients and on the level of confidence they have in their skills and coaching abilities.

Why does one coach charge $350 a month while another coach in the same field charges $1,500, and gets to hand pick his clients? Here's the secret: The second coach simply decides to charge more. If you think you're worth $350 a month, you are. If you think you're worth $1,000 a month, you are. Of course, pricing also depends on other factors, including:

- What your target audience can bear to pay. If you frequently hear, "This is too expensive for me," then you're overpriced. If you never receive objections to your pricing, you're under-pricing your services. If you receive some objections from some prospects, you're priced just right. Generally, coaches who work with executives, professionals, and business owners can charge higher fees.

- Your level of expertise. Obviously, if you've already discovered solutions for people just like them, your clients won't object to higher fees when they compare you to any other coach.

Perceived value is an important factor to consider. Different price points will attract different audiences. At this point in my life, I would never hire a coach who charges less than $750 a month. She might be the best, most experienced coach in the world with a ton of credentials but, *if she doesn't feel she's worth more, why should I?*

It's human nature to judge products and services by the price. The first thing my husband asks if I show him a new outfit is how much I paid. He won't even say whether he likes the outfit until I tell him how much it cost. Flaky? Not really. Most people are like this. Little do they know that pricing is really a marketing strategy.

Taking Your "Energy Costs" into Account

When coaches talk about fees, they often talk in terms of hourly rates. There is one *big* problem with this mentality. When you work with coaching clients, your telephone sessions are not the only time you spend working for the client.

Chances are, you also exchange e-mails with him throughout the week, review notes or other materials between sessions, forward articles or tips he might find useful, and think about his situation while having dinner with your family. Just because the coaching session is over, it doesn't mean your brain has shut down.

A massage therapist can go home and listen to some music after she's done with her client. A hair stylist can change into something more comfortable and relax with a book after seeing her clients.

A coach's mind never stops. We're *always* thinking about our clients' issues and how best to help them. In fact, I come up with some of my best solutions while making dinner! That's why, when you set your fees, you must consider the energy you'll be investing in that client.

Pricing Tiers

I recently attended a live event facilitated by my coach. At the end of the day he invited his private clients to dinner. Before leaving, he turned to the rest of the people and said, "..and the rest of you stay here and contemplate why you're still not in my private coaching club."

Of course, he said it jokingly, but having tiers, or levels of access to you, is very important! This private dinner gave each of us an opportunity to get closer to our coach and get the insights no one else had the privilege to hear.

Create a three-tiered pricing structure, so you can accommodate clients with different budgets and different needs. For example:

Tier 1. Standard Coaching Package: $500 a month includes three 40-minute phone sessions and unlimited e-mails

Tier 2. Advanced Coaching Package: $750 a month includes four 40-minute phone sessions and unlimited e-mails.

Tier 3. Premier Coaching Package: $950 a month includes four 40-minute phone sessions, unlimited e-mails, and review of business plans, strategies and other materials.

In my experience, most clients will opt for the Tier 2 package. This is also true in any other industry – there is a common "not too big, not too small, just right" mentality in most people. Of course, those clients who want to work with the best and get the highest level of access to your coaching will choose Tier 3 package.

If you believe the client will require a lot of time and energy, enroll her into your top-tier package. In fact, you don't even have to mention the other packages. She'll be happy knowing she can send you her documents for review and feedback.

A "coaching club" or another group coaching model is a great way to accommodate clients who want to access your wisdom and support, but don't necessarily want to pay for private coaching. Anyone who wants more individualized coaching—and has the budget for it—can choose one of your high-end programs.

Using Deadlines to Enroll More Clients

I know this is crazy, but time and time again I see people enroll hours or minutes before the deadline, just because they know it's their last chance.

I experienced the true power of deadlines several years ago. My deadline was absolutely real and was necessitated by a valid situation. But thanks to this deadline, I signed up one-third of the participants for my program just hours before it started. To be specific, 150 people signed up for the ACCPOW Coaching Telesummit and about 50 signed up in the final 48 hours–even though everyone had been given a whole month to register!

This was an absolutely phenomenal discovery. I'd always known deadlines were a powerful incentive, but I hadn't realized just *how* powerful they were!

I rarely see coaches use deadlines in their marketing– probably because setting deadlines makes them feel unethical. Many coaches think there's no legitimate reason for setting deadlines. Wrong! There are plenty of valid reasons. Start by considering why people will suffer if they miss your deadline. In other words, what's the logical and legitimate explanation for your deadline? Here are some examples:

1. Group size is limited to ensure that each participant receives individual attention and guidance.

2. There are only so many hours in the day, and you want to work with no more than seven clients. Once all seven spots are taken, you won't be able to take on new clients until next fall.

3. You've just added a bonus to your program, but you're concerned about the time needed to fulfill your promise (e.g., a free personal consultation). You can say something like: "I don't know how long I can offer this bonus because of my personal time involved. If I start feeling overwhelmed, I'll have no choice but remove this bonus. So, if you're planning to sign up, please do it now."

I feel good about every time-limited offer I create because I always have a good reason for it. Always think, "Why should prospects hurry to sign up, or buy my product? What will they lose if they don't sign up in the next 30 days?"

Here's another wonderful approach to increase responses. I call it the "What if you don't sign up today" approach. For example: "What if you don't get a coach today? Are you willing to keep struggling? Are you willing to continue suffering from ADD, or bad time-management, or working at a job you hate?"

This approach makes people *seriously* think about their problems and sources of their pain, so the possibility of quickly eliminating them becomes *much* more appealing.

Final Word on Pricing

Most coaches under price their services. Perhaps they think if priced low enough, more people will be interested in signing up for coaching. I want to challenge you to think differently. What needs to happen for your prospects to sign up regardless of the price? What do they need to see in your marketing materials and on your web site to get a blood rush of excitement and hope?

What I am about to say may sound strange and unfair, but very true. Some of the most successful coaches understand that their programs and products are only as good as their presentation. No matter how good your coaching program is, you will only enroll as many clients as your website copy allows. I am talking about one of the most "taboo" words in the coaching industry–a sales letter.

One of the most important skills you can learn is how to create a no-brainer offer that will enroll clients as if on command. There is nothing magic about copywriting. It's just a matter of studying successful letters and implementing what you learn.

The bad news is that it takes years to get good at copywriting. Some of the most masterful experts charge $10,000-$25,000 per letter!

The good news is that most people never study how to write good copy. So, even if you read only one book on the subject, you'll be way ahead in your industry!

I've summarized everything you need to know about writing an effective copy in the next few pages. If you implement these strategies, your enrollment rate can easily double or triple. (*By the way, if you only read one book on copywriting, it should be Dan Kennedy's "The Ultimate Sales Letter."*)

Creating a No-Brainer Offer

Copywriting is more than 100 years old and many books have been written about the craft. The difference between a good copy and a mediocre one could mean hundreds of thousands of dollars in revenue!

Even though you can hire a freelance copywriter to write your enrollment letter, no one knows your coaching program better than you. I suggest at least writing a rough draft, then letting a freelancer polish it. A good copywriter can suggest creative ways to make your letter more effective. In other words, he or she will help you craft a no-brainer offer!

Here are the time-tested techniques to create copy that attracts and sells:

1 **Write benefits-oriented headlines.** What's the biggest benefit your clients will obtain from working with you? What "huge" problem can you help them solve? This requires that you *really* know your audience and understand what's most important to them. A headline is so important, I actually write 30-40 different ones as a brainstorming exercise before settling on the one I truly like.

Here is a headline Marcia Wieder, one of the most successful life coaches in the country, uses to enroll clients into her program:

"How to Make Your Dreams Come True Any Time You Choose."

Jennifer Koretsky, an ADD coach, clearly explains what her program will help you achieve with this headline:

*"Learn How to Manage Adult ADD and
Move Forward In Life."*

My headlines are usually much longer, because I like to emphasize at least 3 benefits of the program. Here is the actual headline I used to invite people into the program that introduced coaching niches and specialties:

*"Attention Coaches: Do You Want to Quickly Double or
Triple Your Fees, Get A Flood of Client Referrals, and
Become The Leading Coach In Your Field?"*

A good headline will make or break your program's success. I've seen my enrollment triple after a slight revision to a headline. Don't take this lightly–work on your headline until you feel it reflects the #1 benefit your clients will get by going through your program.

2 **Use Attention Grabbers.** Grab attention and lead readers to your page by using an interesting statistic, fact, or story. Then tell them why you do what you do and why YOU are the solution to their problems. Here is an example of a "hook" story I used in one of my enrollment letters:

"There I was, sitting on a bench behind my school, eating bananas. I paid 35 Russian rubles for two bananas–a delicatessen in Ukraine–after standing in line for an hour across the street, and I didn't want my friends to see me. After all, I'd spent my entire stipend to buy them and wasn't going to share. If anyone had told me that years later I'd be living in the U.S., running my own business, making six figures and never wanting to look at another banana, I'd laugh in their face!"

This true story grabs my readers' attention and pulls them in to read further.

Here is a "hook" I used to invite visitors to read more about one of my products:

"They wouldn't let him off the phone... I planned for 35 minutes but what he revealed was so compelling that a bridge line full of people stayed glued to the phone for nearly two solid hours, soaking up every word he had to share."

3 **Stress Benefits in the Text.** List the main benefits of working with you. Begin each list item with a short, snappy statement, and then expand on it with an enticing description. Here are a few examples from a career-coaching program offered by Ford Myers (www.careerpotential.net).

- *You'll discover how to negotiate "like a pro," using the carefully guarded phrases and techniques used only by recruiters, executive agents, and career consultants (until now!).*

- *You'll develop a powerful "Tracking and Organizing System" for all your job search activities, which will consistently boost your productivity, week after week.*

- *You'll understand vital career management strategies that are not taught in school or on the job—but that savvy candidates use to "leapfrog" ahead of even the most qualified people.*

The key to creating powerful benefit "bullets" is using powerful words that create emotion.

4 **Offer Proof.** Provide testimonials from clients and colleagues who've achieved *specific* results (include names and pictures whenever possible). Don't underestimate the power of testimonials! I've purchased many products and services based on testimonials alone!

5 **Include Bonuses.** This is essential! You already have them in your arsenal! Just assemble a "Toolbox" of coaching tools and resources, and create a free bonus. You can make the bonuses time-limited or quantity-limited.

The best bonus you can offer is the one that's closely related to your coaching program. For example, if your program helps new authors get their book in print; actual inquiry letters that got positive responses from publishers would be a huge value-added bonus.

If you coach people in handling conflict in the workplace, an audio CD with sample conflict situations and suggested resolutions would help your clients be more prepared.

Whatever the bonus offer is, it needs to be compelling. I bought several products in the past just because I wanted the bonus!

6 **Make a Guarantee.** Make prospects believe that they're taking *zero* risk by hiring you. This is not to say that you should offer a money back guarantee. Clients just want to know that everything you claim on your web site is true. Obviously, you can't guarantee they'll have the same results some of your other clients experienced; but you can promise that you'll use the same tools, resources, and wisdom to help them achieve similar results. I am strongly convinced that when it doesn't work it's either because you didn't listen, or didn't work hard enough to make it happen.

To simplify the process of writing a "sales letter" or an enrollment letter for your program, let me share with you the nine magic words I recently learned from Mike Litman, the co-author of "Conversations with Millionaires:"

9 Magic Words for Writing Your Copy

1) Tell your story
2) Share your results
3) Sell your system

This formula is so powerful, that any time I feel stuck in writing a sales copy for one of my products, I immediately refer back to it and my writing starts flowing almost effortlessly.

Avoiding Burn-Out

If you have many individual coaching clients right now, I am writing this especially for you.

If you don't have a lot of clients yet, congratulations! This is the best time for you to receive my advice.

Many coaches who fill their practice with one-on-one clients sooner or later "hit a wall." There is no room left for them to grow. Worst of all, they burn out!

I used to be impressed when I heard a coach say, "I've got 20 clients. My practice is full!" Now I think, "The poor thing. He must be exhausted and overbooked, and his clients are probably irritated by his lagging response times."

How do you ensure that this won't happen to you? Remember, those 15 to 20 hours of weekly coaching sessions are not the hours when you're actually working on your business. You must also devote time to administrative and marketing tasks, which you either ignore (at your extreme peril) or perform "after hours."

Here is my formula: Take the number of hours you want to work every week divided by three: 30 hours / 3 = 10 (10 would be the maximum number of coaching clients you should have during any given month). The second 10 hours of your time should be devoted to business development and the remaining 10 hours, on creative strategies. Stay focused on the lifestyle you desire and ask yourself these three questions:

1. Take a look at your current pricing structure. Are you where you want to be? Do you feel resentful toward some clients because you invest more time with them than you want?

2. Have you rejected clients in the past because they can't afford your private coaching fees? Would you take them on if you'd had a group-coaching program?

3. Have you "hit a wall" regarding the number of clients you can handle, as well as the fees you charge? Would it make sense to restructure your coaching business by focusing mainly on a "coaching club" or a coaching community of clients?

I found that I work best when I have a lot of free time and "emotional" space–that is, no deadlines, no pressing projects, and plenty of time to strategize and create. That's why I always limit the number of individual clients to 4-5 at any given time. This allows me to have plenty of "creative energy" to grow my business.

Identifying Problem Clients

Into every coaching business a little rain shall fall–in the form of the problem client. You lose sleep every night, you keep thinking about her project during your lunch, and you feel like your life has been taken over by this client.

Don't you wish you could tell if someone would make your life miserable *before* she became a client? The challenge is to recognize the difficult client when she is still a prospect, and to politely decline her business. How do you do that?

First, define for yourself what "difficult" or "problem" means. It means different things to different people. To decide which factors are most relevant for you, consider these common traits of difficult clients:

- They do not respect your time.

- They tell you how to do your work.

- They always check up on you.

- They constantly change their minds about the project.

- They knit-pick at every detail.

- They try to intimidate you into performing work you never agreed to do (also known as, "project scope creep").

- They treat you as if they're the bosses and you're the employee.

- They have little respect for your expertise.

- They call you at non-scheduled times or after hours.

- They frequently e-mail you with questions that require long replies.

- They keep reminding you that your fees are "high."

- They are frequently disappointed with your work.

- They won't pay on time, but ask you to continue working with them.

- They frequently cancel or reschedule your meetings.

- They don't follow through with their assignments.

- They believe they're your only client and demand your full attention.

I am sure you can extend this list by adding other traits that make dealing with some clients difficult.

It's easy to ignore the early warning signs, or red flags, of a potential problem client, especially if you're hungry for business. But, as one colleague told me, "Your gut is never wrong. Whenever I've ended up with a nightmare client, it's because I didn't listen to my instinct and I went for the zeroes." Listen to your instinct, and watch for these common red flags!

1) The prospect is looking for a quick fix.
2) The prospect doesn't want to sign a contract.
3) The prospect is in a rush.
4) The prospect is looking for the cheapest provider.
5) The prospect is one of your friends or relatives.

Fred Gleeck, one of my favorite authors and speakers, has a very strict screening procedure for his clients. Not only does he ask his potential clients to take a comprehensive personality assessment, he actually makes them pay for it! He then takes a look at the results and makes his decision based on the assessment results. Imagine the desire to work with Fred, if someone is willing to go through this process.

Create a profile of your ideal client in the form of a checklist. Then, after meeting with a prospect, check this person's characteristics against the items on your list.

You might think this is crazy–that choosing clients so carefully will cost you business. Not really. That's because you'll spend more time trying to satisfy the demands of difficult clients than those of your ideal clients (time you could have spent prospecting, working with other clients or simply taking a break). Worse: your mood and personal life may suffer, thanks to this client, and you may not even get paid for the aggravation!

The questions you ask should include things that are important to you as a business owner *and* a person. You may ask how they worked with professionals in the past, what their style of communication is, how much time they plan to devote to the project, what their deadline is, how committed they are to completing it, and so on.

The fact that they're willing to answer an extensive list of questions shows that that they take the project seriously, and it helps you weed out as many "time-wasters" as possible.

Part III: In a Nutshell

1. Offering "coaching services" is very vague to clients. You need to create a coaching program based on your process of working with clients. There are many different models you can choose for your program, depending on your lifestyle and preferences. Choose your coaching model first.

2. You can attract high-paying clients by enhancing your credibility and adding value to your program. Be sure to price your coaching program based on the energy you put into each client's success and the end results they'll experience–not your hourly rates.

3. No matter how good your program is, it is essential to create a no-brainer offer - an enrollment letter that explains its biggest benefits.

4. No more than one third of your time should be spent on coaching clients every week. The rest of your time should be devoted to business development and creative strategies.

5. Screen your clients carefully - a "problem client" will cost you, your business, and your family dearly.

6. The Coaching "Diamond" model helps you create a profit-generating system where you can work with an unlimited number of clients. It is the best way to structure your coaching business for unlimited growth potential.

Part IV
Building Your Market Presence

"Your big opportunity may be right where you are now."
–Napoleon Hill

Survival of the Boldest

If you're already a recognized and celebrated expert in your field, congratulations! If you are a new coach, your situation is different.

When you first become a coach, nobody knows your name. You literally have *zero visibility*. You have no "brand recognition."

I remember how difficult it was for me to fill my first workshop for coaches–only one person registered and I felt embarrassed like never before! Today, thousands of coaches and entrepreneurs know my name, own one or more of my products, and have attended at least one of my events.

I'm not suggesting that your goal is to become a household name like Kellogg's Corn Flakes or Xerox. Few experts become a genuine brand. You *do,* however, need to establish the kind of visibility and credibility that attracts clients to you like you're the only expert in your field.

Unfortunately, many coaches retain zero-visibility status for years after launching their businesses. There are several possible reasons for this:
- They lack confidence in their abilities.
- They think they're not ready for "prime time."
- They are afraid of failing.
- They aren't sure how to identify and "penetrate" a good market.

Today, there are roughly 100,000 coaches in the world. The number is growing fast which is making it difficult to stay ahead of the pack. Only the boldest, most pro-active, and persistent coaches will achieve real success and "rule the world" of coaching! In short, here are the three things that distinguish "rich coaches" from "poor coaches."

1. **Being bold** enough to declare yourself the #1 coach in your field.

2. **Being pro-active** by reaching out to your target audience every day, every week, and every month to increase visibility and generate leads.

3. **Being persistent** to the point that you won't give up, even if your efforts don't produce immediate results.

I built my business mostly through trial and error–the hardest way to do anything. Fortunately, I have learned a lot, so I'll share the best strategies and tactics I've uncovered.

There are many strategies to build a thriving coaching business. If you put me in a room with nothing else to do but to list all the business-building strategies I know, I'd probably spend several hours there and present a 10-page document as a result.

The reality is, you can't do them all. And if you try, you'll end up really frustrated and overwhelmed. One of my clients said to me, "I feel like a huge eighteen-wheeler has been parked in my driveway, with a 300-page driving manual."

You need to choose the strategies that have the highest potential with the least amount of time and money investment. I found some of them to be extremely effective in my own business.

Many coaches already use these strategies in their business but still find themselves struggling to attract clients and customers. What are they doing wrong? And most importantly, how can you avoid their mistakes?

In this part of the book, I am going to dispel many of the myths you hear about web sites, articles, newsletters, teleseminars and joint ventures. There is no right or wrong way here–there is only the way that's been tested to work! The tools and strategies I found to be the most effective in building a coaching business include:

1. **Web Sites** (not your standard brochure-style sites most coaches create);

2. **Articles** (with several important twists to generate a huge number of coaching leads);

3. **Teleseminars** (the quickest way to create value for your clients and attract new ones);

4. **Newsletters** (and a different, less labor and time-intensive way to stay in touch with your subscribers);

5. **Joint ventures** (because you can do much more much faster and with much better results when you partner with others!).

Let's start with the most vital piece of promotional strategy of all–a web site.

"Bottom-Line" Web Sites

If you already have a web site, do you know how successful it is? Be honest. Measure your success by how many people hired you for services or bought your product after visiting it–not by how many compliments you receive.

Most coaching web sites are not profitable. Here is why:

What's the first thing a coach does before launching her own web site? She visits the web sites of other coaches to see what a coaching site *should* look like–the elements it includes, the writing style, the level of detail provided, and so on. Although coaching is a fairly new profession, many standards have already been established for the industry's web sites, including their look and content.

But before you call a web designer to create a "me too" site, ask yourself this important question: How do you know whether another coach's site is successful? Just because it looks great, doesn't mean it generates business. I've seen some really attractive expensive-looking web sites that belong to coaches who are secretly struggling.

It may come as a surprise that most clients will NOT hire you based on your web site alone. Instead, they will visit your web site for one of these four reasons:

1. They received your newsletter or heard about you from satisfied clients.

2. A trusted friend, family member, or colleague recommended you and they want to learn more before calling you.

3. A prospective client wants to confirm your qualifications before hiring you as a coach or a speaker.

4. A customer who purchased your book or another product wants to inquire as to whether you're available for additional support.

5. A search engine user did a specific search and arrived at your web site to read an article you posted there.

In other words, your web site is rarely the first point of contact for a prospective client. And even if it is, there is a very small chance they'll hire you on the spot because of something they saw there.

Wait a minute! You are probably thinking, "Of course they won't hire me on the spot. Coaching is all about building a relationship and bonding and that takes time." At least, that's what everyone has been telling you, right?

In reality, so many coaches have been resisting what I am about to share with you, that it is no wonder so many of their web sites don't bring in revenue. You absolutely *can* get a client on the spot from a first-time visitor to your web site, and I'll show you how in just a moment.

Three Types of Mini-Sites

Most coaches develop a multi-page web site listing their services, bios, articles, testimonials, contact information, etc. These sites are designed to create or increase credibility, and to serve as a "hub" for your other sites. I had a multi-page web site for years and struggled tremendously in trying to get clients. Although such web sites are important, credibility alone does not build a profitable business.

Some coaches discovered a "secret." It's a strategy used by thousands of savvy Internet marketers to generate consistent profits from their web sites. I am talking about *mini-sites*–one to three page web sites that serve just one goal and promote one specific action– whether that action involves an actual sale or generating a lead.

The day I discovered "mini-sites" changed my business forever. Mini-sites are not only much more affordable to create but they can do wonders for your bottom line, as well. Let's take a look at the three types of mini-sites every coach should have.

Each type of mini-site introduced here is an essential element of your business strategy. Your marketing will not be as effective as it could be if you are missing even one of these in your "web site funnel." A web site funnel is series of web sites channeling prospects from one to the next until they enroll in your highest-level, most expensive coaching program.

Mini-Site 1: Get a lead

How big is your mailing list? If you're ever in a room full of marketers, listen to their conversations. One of the most common ways online business-owners measure their success is by the size of their mailing list. Of course, it's better to have a database of 1,500 highly targeted prospects, than a mailing list of 10,000 general contacts, but one thing is clear: without a list, you have no market. That's why having a lead-generating mini-site is absolutely essential for your business!

Here, the goal is to "capture" your prospect's name, e-mail address, and any other information you can encourage him to supply. You can do this by offering an e-course, a special report, a teleseminar recording, or a newsletter–anything that can be delivered instantly using an auto responder[2].

Many lead-generating web sites also sell a product for a small fee to pre-qualify the best prospects. The idea here is that anyone willing to spend a dollar or so for a special report is *much more likely* to spend "real money" on coaching services or additional, and more expensive, informational products.

Whether you give away these products or charge a nominal fee, the materials *must* offer something of high-perceived value–something to help your audience grow their businesses, earn more money, or improve their quality of life. For example, you could interview an ADD expert on "How to Make the Most of Conferences and Training Events if You Have ADD," and you'll have something that any professional or business owner with ADD will want!

Mini-Site 2: Sell a Product

Yes, that's right… Create a one long sales page. Regardless of whether or not you personally like such sites, they work! And if done right, you can create a product-selling web site that makes you feel good.

One of the things I cover with my coaching club members is that a product-selling site should have only ONE link and it should direct clients to your order form. Add another link to the site and you reduce your chances of selling the product by 25%. That's because you'll be taking focus away from your site's SINGLE

---

[2] Auto responder is a web-based program that automatically delivers e-mail messages when triggered by a prospect or by another program.

PURPOSE, which is selling the product. You don't have to believe me: just test it—I did.

My coaching business is product-centered, and if you visit www.milana.com (my "hub" site), you will find many examples of such web sites. Imagine if I had all these products on the same web site–I'd get you so confused and overwhelmed, you wouldn't purchase any of them!

Mini-Site 3: Enroll in a Program

Creating a web site that sells a coaching program designed specifically for your target audience is a "must." This is the type of web site that will allow you to *get a new coaching client on the spot*, although not in the traditional one-on-one coaching format. You must package your coaching services into a program.

Many times, live coaching programs are turned into self-guided programs when they're completed.

You might be saying, "OK Milana, a single-purpose web site is fine for generating leads and selling certain products, but will anyone actually buy *coaching services* after reading my site? When it comes to services, don't most people use web sites for research, and then demand phone conversations or face-to-face meetings to seal the deal?"

The answer is: YES and NO. Yes, they'll want to talk to you in person if you sell "coaching services." But if your site offers a specific, time-limited coaching program, many prospects will enroll on the spot.

Getting More Leads from Your Web Site

As you can see, all three types of mini-site are different, but they focus on one specific action for the prospects to complete:

1. Request a free giveaway

2. Buy a product

3. Enroll in a program

It's important to have all three mini-sites in your coaching business. If you were only going to begin with one, however, I suggest the free giveaway web site is the most important web site to have. This is the web site that collects coaching leads. Remember, without leads, there is no business.

So how do you make a web site that generates massive coaching leads? There are several ways you can do this effectively, but first, let's talk about the three common reasons why a visitor will NOT give you their name and e-mail address:

1. Your visitor simply doesn't want to sign up for anything. She's probably already receiving dozens of newsletters every week. One more newsletter and the big vein on her forehead will pop!

2. Your sign-up form is well hidden within the site. This is a big one! People are already overwhelmed, spending an average of 10 seconds per page. If the sign-up form is not the most obvious thing on your web site, you're losing 55-75% of sign-ups.

3. Your offer doesn't motivate visitors to subscribe. "Join My Mailing List" is a dinosaur, and "Subscribe to My Newsletter" is a sure-fire yawn.

To get someone to give you their name and e-mail, you must create an absolutely irresistible offer they'd be foolish to pass by. Let me give you an example.

I had always wanted to learn about how people make money with "public domain" materials. Basically, you can take a book or a special report whose copyright expired, and sell it as your own for 100% profits. The problem was I had no idea how to get started or where to get those copyright-free materials. Most importantly, I didn't want to get in trouble for selling copyrighted material by mistake.

After doing some online research, I came across an interesting web site. Right there, on the home page, in big bold letters, it said:

FREE SPECIAL REPORT!

"How to Make Money With Public Domain, and The Top 5 Places to Get Copyright-Free Works"

Enter your name and e-mail below to receive this information.

What do I think I did? I immediately entered my information, and "ran" to my e-mail to pick up the copy of this special report.

This was a free offer made by the website owner, and after reviewing it, I couldn't believe my luck. It had the answers to all of my questions and more. Had he offered me a free newsletter, I wouldn't be as interested–I wanted my information instantly!

As a rule, free newsletters and complimentary coaching sessions don't attract much attention. But if your offer:

- Is highly relevant

- Involves interaction

- Helps them solve an immediate problem

- Has something they haven't seen anywhere else

- Or, provides something of high-perceived value…

…They'll sign up!

How do you create an offer that visitors can't refuse? How can you convince them to give you their names and e-mail addresses, even though their inboxes are already overflowing?

Stop and think: What kind of free product–report, article, e-book, special report, or CD–will interest your target audience? What topic would make them stop whatever they were doing and make them think, "I've GOT to have this!"?

The better your free offer, the faster your list of prospects will grow and the more clients you'll have. My web site generates 100 or more new prospects each week and I've seen some people get as many as 1,000 leads a week! Of course, this means that you need a strategy to drive thousands of people to your web site but we'll get to that a little later.

Many people believe that if the offer is free, it doesn't need to be valuable. The truth is, your freebie must be of very high-perceived value to the visitor or he won't bother to sign up.

Let's say you're a career coach. What is the *one* thing your target client wants most? It's to land a well-paying job with excellent growth potential. Therefore, you could create a five- to 10-page report outlining the basics of getting a great job–"10 Insider Secrets of Landing Your Dream Job." How could anyone searching for a career change or new job pass this by! It's free and it's a potentially valuable source of relevant information.

Don't worry about giving away too much in the free report. Do you really think it is possible to cram all of your experience and expertise into just a few pages? No way!

One of my clients created a very unique free offer. His target was the Italian-American community, so he developed a "Top 10 Pick-Up Lines" sheet, featuring his colorful logo and contact information. His web site visitors could easily print it out and slap it on their refrigerators to amuse friends and family. They could also give away copies to their Italian friends.

Another client, a parenting coach, created a *Parenting Toolkit*–a list of steps to follow whenever problems occur. Any time your child misbehaves, you follow these steps to resolve the problem. This was a great way to remind parents about her coaching services.

I recently received a question from a diversity coach who wanted to reach immigrants and foreigners wishing to start a business in U.S. Being a part of this group myself, I immediately suggested that she offer a special report: "Top 10 Secrets Foreigners Must Know About Starting and Running a Business in America." I know many people who would find this information priceless!

Other types of free offers include checklists, worksheets, kits, and e-books. Creating a coaching tool such as a self-test, quiz, or instant assessment can be a great way to convince prospects to give up their contact information! Here are just a few examples of unique self-assessments I've seen created by coaches:

- Five-Star Leadership Test
- "Suddenly Single" Life Makeover
- Anger Management Assessment
- Image Profile Assessment
- Got Debt? Just How Bad Is It?
- Do I Need a Career Coach?
- How Prepared Are You for Your Next Trade Show?
- Do You Live Your Life by Design or by Default?

You could also offer a physical product such as a CD, audiotape, or booklet, but these require time and money to deliver. They don't provide the instant gratification of a download. In the time it takes for prospects to receive your physical product, the excitement about the product may have worn off.

What can you create as a free give-away that will have targeted coaching prospects "lining up" at your web site to request it?

The Truth About Building a Mailing List

One of the most excruciating questions for any web-based business-owner today is how to build a large mailing list. How is it that some people can build a list of 250,000 subscribers in two years (I met a person who has done exactly that!), while others struggle to build a list of a thousand in five years?

I, too, thought there was a mystery or a trick of some kind. After reading hundreds of books, newsletters, and manuals, and talking to some of the most knowledgeable people in the industry, I discovered the secret: It's not about HOW you build a large mailing list - it's about what are you WILLING to do to build it!

In other words, you can be as aggressive or as passive as you wish–the results will show. If you treat list building as a "campaign," by focusing your time and energy for a certain period of time specifically on increasing the size of your list, using all the strategies available to you, it will grow dramatically. There are dozens of strategies you can use including pop-ups, link exchange, co-registration, pay-per-click search engines, online forums, giveaways, blogs, press releases, and affiliate programs, among others.

In fact, Joel Christopher, a very well known marketer, created a whole system for running a mailing list-building campaign that he used to dramatically accelerate the growth of his own list. You can get his strategies at www.coachinglistbuilder.com.

If your efforts are scattered and you only use a couple of methods to build your mailing list, then it will take you much longer.

You'll hear some people say, "It's not about the size of your list–it's about how well it's targeted." This is true: it's much better to have a mailing list of 1,500 financial consultants than a general audience list of 150,000 who have little in common.

Wouldn't it be great, though, if your list was both large and targeted? The bigger and the more targeted your list is, the higher your profit potential is. When I create a new coaching program or a product, the first place I announce it to is my own mailing list. It's a great feeling knowing that I have a highly targeted audience interested in my products and services.

So how do you build a mailing list or a list of coaching leads that may become a list of customers and clients later?

The most effective strategies I've found are writing and submitting articles, and setting up joint ventures–both of which I will share with you next in great detail. These two methods have brought me the best results I've ever seen.

A few other strategies that work very well for many coaches include becoming a columnist in a highly-targeted publication and speaking at industry conventions and conferences. Success for a coaching business is built on trust and credibility so any strategy that allows you to demonstrate these two things will bring high quality coaching leads into your mailing list.

Writing Articles that Bring Coaching Leads

Articles are one of the most powerful yet misunderstood promotional tools for coaches. You don't need to be a "literary giant" or spend hundreds of dollars hiring professional freelancers. Anyone can write an article that brings results. The key is knowing *what results* you want from your articles.

I use articles to accomplish two things in my business:

1. To generate coaching leads

2. To sell my products and programs

Many people write articles to gain credibility and visibility in their industry and that's important, too. But if you are ready to get some tangible results from your writing efforts, you will find the next few pages of this book absolutely priceless!

There are many books and courses that teach you how to write articles. Forget all that–I am going to boil it down to four simple steps for you. Follow them and you'll watch thousands of highly targeted coaching leads flock to your web site.

Earlier we talked about creating a mini-site to collect coaching leads. Now you need to actually bring visitors to your mini-site—you need traffic. One of the most effective ways to do this is by writing articles designed specifically to generate coaching leads. Here are the four simple steps I follow and get amazing results every time:

1. **Choose a topic that represents the #1 reason for your target market's frustration.** For example, if you are a long-term care coach, your target clients deal with a lot of different issues: the financial responsibility of taking care of their elderly family

member; finding the right assisted living center or nursing home; medical coverage; and so on. But if you surveyed a hundred people and asked them, "What is your top concern when it comes to placing your parent into a long-term care facility?" they'd probably say, "Making sure my mom or dad is well taken care of." This is not based on any survey I have conducted but as someone who is dealing with this situation right now, I can tell you that this is the biggest, scariest concern in my family. So, as a long-term care coach, the article topic that will get the most attention from your target audience is something like this:

> *"Ten Steps You Must Take to Prevent Abuse and Mistreatment of Your Loved One in a Long Term Care Facility."*

2. **Create a list of 7-10 steps, ways, or strategies to solve this frustration.** The easiest format for a how-to article is a list of steps or tips. A narrative format is ok, but the step-by-step approach is a lot more practical for publishers and valuable to readers. Each step or tip should come with an example or explanation. Here is an illustration:

> *"Do your research before committing to a long term care facility. Find out what their aide-to-patient ratio is, how they screen their employees, and whether there is a patient advocate on staff. There are also places on the Internet where you can get the ratings for most of the long-term care facilities in the U.S., so be sure to request a rating report before making your final decision."*

3. **Add a resource box to your article.** Traditionally, a resource box includes the name and contact information of the author. These resource boxes are highly ineffective for your purpose: bringing you a coaching lead. The only thing that will bring thousands of readers to your web site is something enticing

and *FREE*. For example, any time I write an article about using assessments as a business tool, my resource box looks like this:

> *"Milana Leshinsky is a business advisor to coaches and independent professionals. Get a copy of her FREE report called "How to Create Self-Assessments and Quizzes that Bring Clients, and Keep Them Coming Back!" at http://www.assessmentgenerator.com"*

4.   **Submit your article to highly relevant newsletters, magazine publishers, article submission web sites, and depositories.** Don't let your article "collect dust" on your hard drive–get it out there! Pull out the list of highly targeted newsletters you found during your market research and e-mail your article to every publisher. Send it as an attachment and write a brief letter to the publisher. Here is the actual letter I used to have one of my articles published:

> *"Hi Will,*
>
> *Do you accept articles for your "Coaching Compass" newsletter? I am sending you an original freshly written article titled, "Thrive or Starve: Every Coach's Sticky Situation," and hope you can use it. Please, see attached.*
>
> *Thank you so much,*
> *Milana Leshinsky, Business Advisor to Coaches*
> *http://www.milana.com*
>
> *P.S. If you find this article of high quality and would like to receive more articles on coaching practice building, practice management, or creating passive income sources in the future, let me know. I will send them to you hot off the press!"*

Will Craig published a shortened version of the article in the "Coaching Compass," a popular publication for coaches, bringing hundreds of new subscribers and client leads into my mailing list.

As you can see, these four steps are very straightforward and easy to follow. You can have your article written in just a couple of hours and submit it to publishers the same day!

Recently, I discovered a new way to enhance my articles, which greatly intensified their impact. I put a twist on my articles–a coaching twist!

Articles with a Coaching "Twist"

I came to understand two crucial things about articles:

a) My most desired response from every article was to generate a *lead*. I used to think it was to make a sale but I was wrong.

b) The standard "resource box" doesn't work. People read the article, but don't click through to my web site. I needed something much stronger to pull readers into my web site.

Once I realized this, I tried something different. I wrote an article entitled *"Why Most Coaches and Consultants Have a Limited Income Potential and What to Do About it."* The basis for the article was Michael Gerber's book *The E-Myth*, where he introduced the concept of working ON your business, as opposed to IN your business. At the end of the article, I included a link to a self-test: *Do you work IN your business or ON your business?*

The results: Eight of 10 readers clicked on the self-test link. Five of 10 actually took the test, and at least 500% more people expressed interest in my products and services. People read the article, clicked on the link to the self-assessment, and gave me their contact information.

I achieved similar success with my next article, *Is Your Product or Service an "Ideavirus"?* It was based on Seth Godin's book, *Unleashing the Ideavirus*, and consisted of two parts: an article and an assessment. First, I explained what "ideavirus" meant. Then I recommended an assessment to help readers determine whether their own product is an "ideavirus." (See the actual article and assessment in *Appendix B*.)

Following publication, people started telling their friends about my self-tests! My list was growing twice as fast as before. Every article generated dozens of leads in the first few days, and hundreds more over the next few months. I'd found the ULTIMATE article writing strategy!

You can achieve the same results by using this strategy in your own business. Review the articles you've already written and decide which ones could be enhanced with a self-test or an assessment, and then re-publish it.

Writing Articles that Sell a Product

Lead-generating articles are a key way to increase your exposure and the size of your subscriber list. But wouldn't you also like to generate revenue from every article you write? I am not talking about selling your articles to magazines. Let me explain.

I used to write about anything related to my expertise, and while these articles were usually published, they did not produce any significant results. I would get a lot of great feedback, compliments, and exposure, but no sales.

Then, in August 2002, adding to my three e-books, I wrote an article entitled *How to Make Money on the Internet without Creating Your Own Product.*

The article explained how to buy reprint rights to someone else's product and turn it into a profitable business. It included all the details about how to find a high-quality product, questions to ask the author, and other important tips. My hope was that people would read the article, and then go to my web site to buy the rights to my own e-books.

Over the next three months, I received over a hundred inquiries and sold a half-dozen reprint rights packages, ranging from $400 to $2,500–all from a single 1100-word article. If my math is right, that's approximately $5,000 of revenue generated from just one article.

Why did it work? What did I do right?

I believe six things made the difference:

1. I had a <u>specific goal in mind</u>–to sell reprint rights to my e-books. In other words, I knew what my end result should be *before* writing the article.

2. I wrote a detailed <u>step-by-step guide</u> on this topic. By doing this, I demonstrated my knowledge and expertise on this topic.

3. I introduced <u>my own products as an example</u>. Using my products as a case study allowed me to sell without selling.

4. I <u>linked to the page</u> where I sold reprint rights. In other words, I told readers where they could obtain the rights to the products used in the case study. Again, selling without selling.

5. I submitted the article to <u>dozens of targeted online publications</u> and they loved how content-rich it was. Nobody questioned that I was using my own products as an example because it was highly educational.

6. I placed the article on <u>my web site</u>, adding a title and keywords, so that search engines would "pick it up."

In other words, this was not just *any* article. It was a strategic and educational marketing piece. Even though I stopped selling reprint rights to my e-books years ago, the inquiries still come in on a regular basis.

The most important point I want you to understand about this strategy is this: first, decide on the product or program you want to promote, then write your article – not the other way around. This will allow you to naturally and organically tie your article to your product.

Make Your Newsletter Pay

If you're already publishing a newsletter, but haven't seen any significant results, you're not alone!

Month after month, thousands of coaches sit down at their computers, write a newsletter filled with articles, tips and resources, and send it to their mailing lists. They do this every month, even though these newsletters bring in little or no business. Why? Because that's what everyone else is doing–because newsletters are a standard tactic for staying in touch with prospects in the hope of sooner or later converting them into clients. Unfortunately, it's usually later–if ever.

I've been publishing newsletters since 2001. I've tried different formats, lengths, styles, content and frequencies. In other words, I struggled and I experimented.

In the process, I discovered the secrets of why one newsletter generates revenue every time it's published while others generate nothing. Here they are:

Four Elements of creating Profitable Coaching Newsletters

1 **Personality.** This is the defining factor! Nothing can be a greater waste of time than publishing a generic newsletter with no personality. It's easy to spot a newsletter without personality. Just look for the word "I"–and you probably won't find it there. Remember, coaching is a personal and intimate experience. Injecting your voice into the newsletter helps readers identify with you as a person and a professional.

If you're not sure whether your newsletter has any personality, ask a friend and your spouse to read it. Can they "hear" your voice as they read it? Can they tell you wrote it? If the answer is yes, then it has personality!

On the other hand, if the newsletter reads like an excerpt from an Associated Press story, re-write it in your own voice. Start by rewriting one article, then reading it out loud. Does it read the way you normally speak? Do you normally sound excited, gentle and understanding, quick and to the point, or inspiring? Insert your voice into your newsletter, and ideal prospects may soon become your biggest fans!

As Dr. Seuss says, "Be who you are and say what you feel, because those who mind don't matter, and those who matter don't mind."

2 **Relevancy.** Nature, movies, travel, music, and family are all great topics but are they relevant to your coaching specialty? If not, write about something you normally teach clients. If you're a relationship coach, there are GAZILLIONS of things you can write about–from choosing the perfect partner to issues with the in-laws. Best of all, when you choose a topic relevant to your business, you'll have a ready supply of real life examples, case studies, illustrations, and tips!

Publishing a newsletter that's relevant to your expertise will not only retain and increase your readership, but will encourage prospects to approach you directly.

3 **Focus.** I've noticed many coaches include bits and pieces of information, a couple of short "how to" articles, a longer feature story, and sidebars containing tips and resources. This is *not* an effective format for a newsletter, in terms of generating leads and sales. The most effective newsletter focuses on a single topic per issue. Include tips and resources if you'd like, but place the focus on a *single* topic in every newsletter.

If your goal is to generate revenue, each issue should be treated like a sales letter–one goal, one recommended product–period. It should be highly informative or educational but it should be focused on one specific issue.

If you include multiple links in your newsletter, you'll dilute your results. I've tested this dozens of times and the result is always the same: one article with a single link to a recommended product generates 7-10 times more sales than an issue that looks like the front page of *USA Today*.

4 **Call to Action.** This is the biggest failing of coaching newsletters. Great topic, great information, plenty of personality, and a unique voice... but no call to action! A call to action is your recommended step to the reader–her next move to implement the ideas you've just shared with her. Ideally, you will tie everything you write into a coaching program or a product. For example, going back to relationship coaching, an action step could be:

- Take a self-assessment on marriage readiness.
- Sign up for a "communication for couples" teleseminar.
- Register for an upcoming group-coaching program for couples.
- Attend a live event on love and dating.
- Purchase a book or audio program on family budgeting.
- Submit a question about your relationship.

These calls to action either prompt a purchase or encourage further interaction with you, which gets your reader one step closer to becoming a client. Without a call to action, your subscribers will read your stuff, mentally thank you for the information, and file it away. Make sure that every issue you publish contains a simple call to action.

If You Still Don't Get Results...

"Hey, I do all of that! Why don't I get coaching clients from my newsletter?" If that's what you're thinking, please re-read the four factors more closely. You might have missed something. If you truly are implementing these four factors, there may be two additional reasons why your newsletter isn't generating satisfactory results:

1. Your mailing list is too small. If you have fewer than 1,000 people on your list, it may take a longer to generate clients from your newsletter. Build your list to at least 3,000 to consistently generate new business.

2. Your mailing list is not targeted enough. Do the people on your list share common challenges and concerns? If your list is very diverse, it may be difficult to (a) choose a good topic to write about, and (b) get readers interested enough to take action.

Many business owners choose not to publish a newsletter. I stopped publishing mine a little over a year ago. Why? My answer is very simple–it took too much time. I had to spend at least 5-6 hours every month writing, assembling, and sending it to my subscribers, while getting nominal results.

It simply didn't work for my lifestyle, so I discontinued it. This is not to say that I am not in touch with my subscribers. I replaced my newsletter with an automatically delivered e-course (a series of lessons sent to prospects via e-mail) followed by occasional articles, tips, and announcements to my mailing list.

The choice is yours but whatever you do, make a decision based on your goals and results–not on what others are doing.

Teleclasses - Turning Participants into Clients

Imagine sitting on your porch and watching your kids play in the backyard. At the same time, you are holding a telephone and talking to 20 people from other states, Canada, Australia, UK, and other places all over the world. Modern technology makes this possible!

Teleseminars, also known as teleclasses, are a great way to get new coaching clients and sell your products. Originally, teleconferencing was used in the corporate world and later, for distant learning purposes. Now, every savvy marketer and entrepreneur uses teleseminars to grow their business.

Many people talk about building your brand and making money with teleseminars. In case you're new to this, let me give you a quick crash course.

Teleclasses are a fun way to connect with other like-minded people, learn a new skill and pick up some useful information. Everyone dials the same conference line, also called a bridge line, and listens to the class leader.

Some teleclasses are interactive, where participants are encouraged to ask questions and share ideas. Although teleclasses are extremely powerful, very few coaches successfully use them to gain new clients. It's all in the planning and knowing exactly what to do. Here's how you can enroll more coaching clients from teleclasses, every time. Start by dividing your Teleclass "campaign" into three stages:

1. **Before**
2. **During**
3. **After**

Each stage is equally important. Let's take a look at what each stage involves and how you can ensure success every time you hold a teleclass.

BEFORE TELECLASS

The success of your teleclass will hinge largely on your preparation for the event, including:

1) Developing a mailing list of targeted prospects for your coaching business.

2) Choosing a problem or set of problems that you specialize in solving.

3) Creating a well-written, benefits-oriented enrollment web page, with your photograph and a user-friendly sign-up form.

4) Offering a content-rich handout with case studies, tips, and links to your web site with some space to write in.

5) Developing a coaching program curriculum (group-based or one-on-one) to use as the "back end" for your teleclass. In fact, it's best to hold a free Teleclass three or four weeks before your program begins.

6) Sending at least three reminders about your Teleclass to increase participation.

Here are some examples of teleclasses that were very well received because of their specific audience and "hot" topic:

- "Sharing Custody With a Jerk"
- "How to Stop Your Divorce"
- "5 Steps to Making it Big in the Publishing Business"

DURING TELECLASS

Here's where your preparation will really pay off:

1) Stick to your handout and discuss the case studies you prepared.

2) Devote 75% of the Teleclass to content and 25% to questions and group discussion.

3) Mention your coaching program about halfway through the teleclass and again at the end.

4) Mention any tools you're using with your clients to help them identify problems and areas to work on.

5) Invite participants to take advantage of a special coaching offer–a discount, a bonus, a resource, etc.–available *only* if they enroll in your coaching program by a certain date.

AFTER TELECLASS

Don't take a vacation just yet. It ain't over 'til it's over and you start seeing deposits in your bank account!

1) Send an immediate thank-you note to all Teleclass participants with an audio "replay" link.

2) Send a follow-up e-mail featuring class notes, resources, and information about your coaching program.

3) Send another follow-up with the deadline to enroll in your coaching program, including testimonials from past clients.

4) Send a final mailing to those who still haven't enrolled to let them know when you will run the program in the future, and to inform them about other products or services that you offer.

Yes, I know this comprises four mailings! But most people are procrastinators and need a gentle nudge. They may enroll in your program just hours before it begins, but they'll be extremely thankful that you didn't give up on them!

In ALL of the above, the most important step is establishing a *back-end coaching program* to which you'll invite Teleclass participants. Do you have a time-defined program? Does it offer a specific curriculum? Does it include bonus materials? Does your web site offer the coaching program using a "sales letter" page with an "Enroll Now" button? All of this must be in place before the teleclass to increase your sign-ups.

I was recently on a teleclass, which resulted in dozens of participants enrolling into a "high-ticket" full-blown coaching program. This was a free teleseminar with Michel Fortin, one of the top copywriting experts. He discussed various strategies he has been using to increase sales from his web sites.

Michel's ultimate goal for the teleseminar was to enroll people into his paid program. As I listened, my excitement grew with every minute. By the end of the call, I was ready to sign up! In fact, if it weren't a $2,000 event (plus airfare and almost a week away from my kids), I would have whipped out my credit card!

When the teleseminar was over, I asked myself, "What made me feel so excited and pumped up about this?" Well, here's what Michel did to make me feel this way:

Somewhere in the middle of the call, he started naming specific results that I would achieve by attending his event. He also turned testimonials into case studies, examples into exciting stories.

Most coaches are taught to ask, "When would you like to start our first session?" or "What did you think of today's call?" or "How would you like to experience this every week?" Instead, excite your prospect with potential results. Provide examples and illustrations, ask questions, and let the prospect ask YOU if you can coach her. Of course, you don't want to give any guarantees, but if they feel that your guidance has helped other clients achieve great results, they'll trust that you can help them, too.

My Recipe for Joint Venture Success

Personally, I love working alone. Peace and quiet allow my brain to be much more creative and productive than if I am surrounded by people. Many times, however, I find it crucial to connect and work with other business owners, especially joint venture (JV) partners.

As coaches, we have a huge advantage when it comes to creating joint ventures: we are all experts on something! We can develop and offer seminars, business tools and coaching programs—things that many business owners can't do. Yet, just 7% to 10% of coaches actually establish strategic alliances, and only 2% do so successfully.

Here's what some clients have told me when I asked why they weren't partnering with other people:

- "Strategic alliances are for big companies; I'm too small!"
- "I have nothing to offer to them."
- "They're way out of my league."
- "I don't want my business to get too big and out of control!"
- "My mailing list is too small."

Believe me when I say: None of these answers should stop you from creating a joint venture. I've partnered with people "bigger" than me, "smaller" than me, and with start-ups. Each had something I wanted, such as:

- A special expertise
- A large mailing list
- A unique idea
- Credibility in the community
- A special resource

A joint venture is a deal between two or more companies designed to advance and accelerate the growth of each other's business.

You don't *need* to partner with another person or company, but joint ventures are a *much* more effective use of your time and resources. Joint ventures help you *cost-effectively* expand your markets, and offer new products and services to your clients.

You also gain *fast* access to resources and talent in ways you never could by yourself. For example, alone, it would've taken me months or years to develop several products and events that my joint venture partners helped me create in just a few weeks! In many cases, I wouldn't have even created them at all.

Anything you can accomplish through a joint venture can be accomplished on your own. But, it takes longer, costs more money, and you might never get the reach or resources to complete them.

Joint venturing is also the first and most important strategy I recommend to new coaches who just created a product or developed a coaching program.

So how do you make joint ventures work in your business and bring in amazing results?

In the next few minutes, I will share with you the six elements of the most effective joint ventures I've ever put together. Depending, of course, on your field, you may consider other elements.

Six Elements of Effective JVs

At least 50% of my business has been built using joint ventures and strategic alliances. I strongly believe that without my joint venture partners, my bank account would be much "leaner."

In my experience, there are six key ingredients that will almost guarantee a successful partnership:

1. The same target audience.
2. At least one party must have the mailing list.
3. At least one party must have the expertise.
4. Each partner must feel he's getting the better part of the deal.
5. Both partners must be equally passionate and committed to making the joint venture work.
6. Think long-term.

Let's take a look at each one in detail.

1 **The same target audience.** There is rarely a basis for a partnership without the same target market. Make sure you partner with people who target the same customers and clients as you do. For example, one of the joint ventures I created with my partner, Suzanne Falter-Barns, was "Licensing Revenue Secrets."

We knew that people who develop information products, workshops, seminars, and other intellectual property would be interested in learning how to license them. My target audience was coaches, while Suzanne worked with coaches, authors, and speakers. It made sense for us to partner in co-creating a "how-to" product on licensing because it appealed to both of our target markets.

2 **At least one party must have the mailing list.** You must share at least one existing database of prospects, whether you're going to promote a new product or an existing one. In the case of the "Licensing Revenuc Secrets," both Suzanne and I had mailing lists–the key to having a strong promotional strategy.

3 **At least one party must have the expertise.** You absolutely must have a specialized expertise on which to base the joint venture, or you might end up in a "blind-leading-the-blind" situation. While my expertise on licensing was sketchy, Suzanne sold her workshops for over two years with much success, and had a lot of tips and strategies to incorporate into the product.

4 **Each partner must feel he's getting the better part of the deal.** That's a given. Not only must a joint venture be mutually beneficial, but your partners should feel they're getting the "longer end of the wishbone." For example, I wanted to create the product on licensing, but didn't have enough information about it. Partnering with Suzanne would allow me to have a ready-to-sell product without having to learn all nuts and bolts about licensing.

What was in it for Suzanne? She would also get a ready-to-sell product and a new source of passive income. Additionally, I was responsible for all the logistics (recording and producing the CDs) as well as promoting it to my large database of customers and subscribers. Each of us got something we didn't have without this partnership.

5 **Both partners must be equally passionate and committed to making the joint venture work.** Estimate how much work is involved and who will handle each aspect of the project. If one partner loses excitement and stalls, the entire venture could fail, leaving both parties unhappy. The key to mutual satisfaction is planning and making the commitment. I knew that writing a "sales letter" to sell the product was a huge chunk of work, but I considered it my responsibility in this partnership and delivered. On the other hand, Suzanne knew that I had very little knowledge of licensing at the time, and ended up creating most of the content herself.

6 **Think long-term.** One successful project can lead to many more in the future. In fact, it should! Finding the right partner isn't always easy, but when you find a good match, you'll want to keep working with that partner for as long as it makes sense. I have several joint venture partners, with whom I collaborated again and again. Any time I get an idea for a new product or program, my joint venture partners are the first people that come to mind. It's a wonderful feeling to know that I don't have to have all the answers!

Case Study: A Win-Win-Win Joint Venture

When Jo Romano, the owner of the Lawyer's Life Coach Company, approached me with an idea for a Worldwide Coaching Mastery Telesummit on Niches and Specialties, I was still "recovering" from a telesummit I'd conducted the previous month. Could I handle another event of this caliber so soon? Absolutely not.

But when she said, "I'll do all the work—you just coach me through the process," I decided to accept. Basically, she said the "magic words!"

I ended up doing a bit more than coaching, but ultimately, we assembled 152 new coaches from around the world and made a huge splash, presenting 11 of the hottest coaching niches and specialties—a topic of much debate and controversy.

Here's why this proved to be a win-win-win joint venture.

1. Jo used my company's name to increase the credibility of her event, she received a free personal mentor for two months (me), and she connected with some of the biggest names in the coaching industry.

2. I was able to leverage the idea of a "telesummit," so more people today understand and are excited about attending a week-long event via telephone. I earned 50% of the net profits from the event, and created a new, high-quality product with very little effort.

3. The customers were winners, too. Many coaches are still searching for the ideal niche, so teaching our participants about the 11 most important and exciting specialties provided them with the "nudge" needed to make their decision.

Getting Started With Joint Ventures

Now that you have seen how joint ventures work, how do you approach someone about a joint venture? How do you write a proposal that blows them away? How do you make them feel that this is their lucky day? I came up with this formula for pitching JV proposals, and it has worked for me 99% of the time.

1. Establish your credibility.
2. Tell them what's in it for them.
3. Explain your idea briefly.
4. Tell them how to get started.

I once sent an invitation to Joel Christopher, asking him to speak at my coaching telesummit. At the time, I thought, "There's no way I'll get him to say YES. He's just too big." Joel had been in business for years and had spoken at dozens of high-profile seminars. When I launched my business more than five years ago,

Joel's name was all over the Internet. He was considered the biggest expert on building big mailing lists. To my amazement, he accepted the invitation. What's more, we established a great relationship, soon met in person, and I'm sure we'll do more business in the future.

Setting up joint ventures is fun *and* simple! Here are the action steps you can take right now to create your own partnership:

Action Steps to Create a Joint Venture

Step 1: Make a list of five types of companies that target the same customers as you. For example, if your target audience is newly married couples, then your potential joint venture partners may include attorneys, financial advisors, real estate agents, and relationship experts.

Step 2: List five people you know in each of those businesses–people you've met online, at events, or your customers and affiliates.

Step 3: Study their web sites, products, and services to gain insight into what they're looking for.

Step 4: Develop a joint venture idea so beneficial to THEM; they won't be able to refuse! Be creative!

To be fair, I should mention that many times, you will never hear back from a prospective joint venture partner. Don't despair! Just move on, with a better idea and a different partner!

Some joint ventures will require you to be flexible. I recently had to negotiate a partnership with one of the top business owners in my industry. It took weeks, and just as I was ready to call it quits, we found a way to make it work for both of us. Had I not been flexible and patient, I would've missed an opportunity to generate thousands of dollars in revenue and add hundreds of targeted names to my mailing list.

Joint ventures can work magic for both business coaches and life coaches. You might need just one joint venture to bring your business to a completely new level of success!

Final Word About Marketing And Self-Promotion

Many coaches believe that their expertise should speak for itself. They know they're good and feel it's beneath them to engage in marketing and selling. Most successful coaches, however, believe that no business is possible without marketing.

If you find yourself struggling with the idea of marketing, self-promotion, and the negative connotation it has in the coaching world, consider what T. Harv Eker said in his *"Secrets of the Millionaire Mind*:

> "If you believe that what you have to offer can truly assist people, it's your duty to let as many people as possible know about it. In this way, you not only help people, you get rich!"
>
> T. Harv Eker

Any time people buy your products or services, they are buying YOU. There is no one else like you in the world. You are unique and thousands of people are waiting to experience your wisdom and unique message.

Personally, I don't know a single coach or an entrepreneur who achieved success without having a strong self-promotional mindset. I urge you to release any negative emotions about marketing, and you will see a whole new level of energy, excitement, and success in your business!

Part IV: In a Nutshell

1. With 30,000 coaches and 200+ coach training schools in the world today, only the boldest, most pro-active, and persistent coaches will succeed in their chosen fields.

2. The top five strategies you should use to penetrate your niche market include web sites, articles, teleseminars, newsletters, and joint ventures.

3. Mini-sites are the most powerful kind of coaching websites. Every coach should have three mini-sites: to get a lead, to sell a product, and to enroll prospects into a coaching program.

4. To generate coaching leads in large numbers, you need to create an irresistibly attractive free giveaway. A newsletter alone will not attract leads.

5. Writing articles must always have a purpose. The two main article goals are a) to bring a lead, and b) to sell a product or program.

6. There are four main elements in every successful newsletter: personality, relevancy, focus, and call to action.

7. When holding your teleseminar, you must think of all three stages: before (planning), during (execution) and after (follow-up). All three are equally important for converting participants into customers or clients.

8. Every successful joint venture depends on six key elements: target audience, mailing list, expertise, a win-win deal, commitment, and long-term opportunities.

9. Business coaches are considered a necessity, while life coaches are often considered a luxury. That's why life coaches must "create" their own clients.

10. You must consistently market your coaching business. This is the only way to experience the level of success I know you want.

Part V
Passive Coaching Income

"A project is complete when it starts working for you, rather than you working for it."
— Scott Allen

The Move to Passive Coaching Income

Do you ever wish you could take a vacation from coaching–not because you *need* a vacation, but because you'd *like* one? Whether you offer one-on-one coaching, group coaching, workshops, or seminars, you're involved in ACTIVE coaching. You must physically show up to get paid.

Wouldn't it be great if you could travel to the Bahamas, Bermuda or Alaska for a week (just for the heck of it) and return to a healthy revenue stream? You can if you set up passive coaching income sources.

Many coaches have certain misconceptions about creating passive income sources and why going "passive" might hurt their "real" coaching business. Let me address some of these issues here.

Income "Ceiling"

When you coach one client at a time, you'll quickly reach your capacity–in terms of time and energy, both mental and physical. Therefore, your income will be limited to the number of clients multiplied by fees. Many coaches believe they need to justify their hourly or monthly fees by working harder, which places even more pressure on them.

Coaches Are in the Information Business

One of the ways to earn passive income is through creating and selling information products, such as electronic books, audio programs on CDs, home-study courses, and other educational materials. High-paying clients are attracted to the coach who "walks the walk" *and wrote the book.* In other words, demonstrating your expertise via info-products will catapult you into the top 5% of coaches in your field.

Passive Income Phenomenon

When it comes to passive verses active coaching income 80/20 actually equals 50/50. You may spend 20% of your working hours coaching clients, and 80% of your time creating products, but your income will actually be split 50/50 between these two revenue sources.

For example, let's say that you make $50,000 a year coaching clients one day per week, spending the rest of your time creating passive income sources. It's highly likely that $25,000 of your revenue will come from products, and the other $25,000 from coaching clients. Why? Because your products confer credibility that will attract motivated, high-paying clients who will be honored to work with you! Instead of making $450 a month per client, you'll earn $750 - $1,500 a month while working less!

Reaching the Point of Not Needing Clients

Working on your passive income strategies doesn't mean you have to stop coaching. You can continue to coach clients even when you're generating passive income. The only difference is that you won't just be coaching for money; you'll be doing it for the gratification and professional development that comes with coaching.

Thomas Leonard, the founder of Coachville and Coach University, and creator of many concepts and models used by coaches worldwide, once wrote, "Start the shift to passive revenue sources, even if you have a thriving practice and love your time with clients."

The problem I usually see in making the shift is the need for immediate cash flow. If a client comes along and you need the money, you'll accept the business. This leaves less time and energy for creating your passive income sources. If you don't have enough passive income, you continue to take on individual clients to earn a living. The cycle repeats over and over again... until you finally decide to do something about it.

You don't have to depend on the income from your individual clients. You can easily generate revenue even while you're away from your business. Here are the nine steps to take for breaking the cycle:

1. Leverage everything you do. Save everything you say, write or create, and turn them into products at a later date.

2. Raise your fees. This will allow you to "filter" some clients, keeping only the ones who are highly motivated to work with you.

3. Be very selective when it comes to taking on new clients. Create a list of criteria that represent your "ideal client," and stick to it.

4. Create coaching groups for most of your clients.

5. Pre-qualify your free-session candidates by asking them to complete a questionnaire.

6. Whenever you reply to a client's e-mail, save it in a "special idea file." In this way, you'll begin stockpiling your intellectual property for later use.

7. Save any tools, worksheets, checklists or templates you create for clients.

8. "Fire" any clients you no longer enjoy working with.

9. Spend at least one day each week developing passive income streams.

You don't have to perform all 9 steps at once. Pick a few with which you're comfortable TODAY and get them started. Then, re-assess your business situation within 30 days, and determine if you can implement more of these steps.

Using these strategies will help you break free from "needing" clients and shift into a completely independent business with many income sources possibilities.

Three Passive Income Strategies

Which words or phrases best describe your current cash flow situation?

- From time to time
- It depends
- With a little luck
- Steady, predictable and consistent

There was a time when I could never predict my income. One month I would work with one coaching client and sell twenty CDs. Another month, I might work with five clients and sell only seven CDs. My income kept fluctuating depending on how much marketing I did that month, on how many teleseminars I conducted, or on how productive my affiliates were. When I discovered the concept of a passive and residual income, I couldn't believe what I was missing!

Creating multiple sources of coaching income will help you build a strong and steady financial base, and allow you to stop worrying about how many clients you have or how many people attend your workshops.

I've identified three types of income that coaches generate: (1) Truly Passive; (2) Leveraged; and (3) Residual. You may see some overlap here, but there are also certain distinctions I want you to understand.

Before I continue, however, here's a word of caution: Do not attempt the following strategies unless you've already identified your niche. Without a niche, you'll find yourself struggling and frustrated, no matter what you do.

TRULY PASSIVE

Truly Passive income is an income source that is established once, and marketed through the same strategies you're already using for your business. For example:

- E-books and other downloadable products
- Audio programs (as MP3 files or audio CDs)
- Home-study courses and manuals

LEVERAGED

Leveraged income sources are created from existing content and resources and translated into different formats with different price points. Basically, the content is created once, then re-used and re-purposed over and over again. Here are just a few examples of how information can be converted from one format to another to maximize your income:

- Client support e-mails turned into articles
- Articles turned into workshops or electronic books
- An electronic book turned into a teleseminar
- A teleseminar turned into coaching program

Another type of leveraged income lets you make money while others do the work.

- Jointly created products (joint ventures)
- Jointly created promotions (strategic alliances)
- Selling products through an affiliate program
- Licensing your materials to others

| **RESIDUAL** | Residual Income occurs over time from work done once. This offers the highest potential income source of all. For example: |

- Membership-based coaching programs (e.g., coaching club)
- Subscription web site (e.g., online community)
- Reseller commissions from subscription services (e.g., shopping cart service, auto responders, and other membership sites that pay affiliate commissions)

Another great way to earn passive revenue is by licensing your materials to others. These may include workshops, training programs, books, workbooks, and any other intellectual property you developed. You can make your "turnkey" licensing package attractive by including marketing materials, worksheets, facilitation tips, and other helpful information.

While each income type is important, a combination of all three creates *predictable* sources of income from your business.

If you're feeling overwhelmed by looking at all these strategies, please remember: you don't have to understand any of the technical details behind creating your products and web sites. There are many people out there who can help you set it all up.

Later in the book, you'll learn about how using a Virtual Assistant in your business can save you countless hours, days and weeks of frustration! They've been trained to support professionals just like you in technology, customer service, and administrative tasks of your business.

In the next few sections, I will show you how you can quickly and easily create your products and membership web sites, and how to bring it all together to create a highly lucrative coaching business.

Creating Your First Product

I was lucky enough to stumble upon Ken Evoy's "Make Your Knowledge Sell" early on in my business. I literally "swallowed" this book and three months later, I had my first product to sell. I was excited and couldn't wait to see what would happen next.

I completed my e-book on January 15. The first order came on February 26, from Andrew Smith (it's funny how you remember your first customer–I had his receipt printed out and framed over my computer for months!). My product was an e-book called "Create Your First Business Web Site in 10 Days!" and it felt like I'd just poured all my knowledge of web design into those 129 pages.

Six months later, I wrote another e-book for more advanced web site designers and within another few weeks, I wrote my third e-book on some of the most advanced web development strategies.

Here is an interesting observation: My very first e-book took me over three months to write, my second e-book was finished within six weeks; and my third e-book was whipped out in literally a few hours! I learned the process and felt like I could do this with my eyes closed, over and over again.

The problem was, I didn't have a "back-end." Each e-book sold for about $27, and generated a total of $1,500-$2,000 a month, but I couldn't raise my income any higher because I offered nothing in terms of implementation support.

As I began working in the coaching industry, I realized what I had missed. With my own products, I could not only add another source of income to my business, but to also dramatically increase my credibility and visibility in the community.

Most importantly, product sales help pre-qualify coaching prospects. If someone's willing to spend $20 for your book, he's *already* expressed an interest in your expertise, and has moved closer to becoming your client. Products can transform "warm" prospects into "warmer" ones. As soon as I began offering "back-end" consulting and web design services to my customers, my income went up.

One more note about products: every successful coach offers them–books, audio programs, manuals, workbooks, e-books, private web sites…you name it. Many of them develop a whole line of products packaged together or sold separately. They all use products to make money at the back of the room during speaking events, and even send them to editors and producers to publicize their products and services.

I found some very effective ways to develop new products fast. If you've been procrastinating and finding excuses not to create a product, these strategies will empower you for years to come!

If you're a brand new coach or have never created a product, you can easily–almost effortlessly–create your first coaching product by following these tips:

Put Yourself In Product Creation Mode

Everything you write or speak about should be turned into a product. If it only has one use, don't do it.

Re-Purpose Your Articles

Do you already write articles to promote your web site? If so, you can use them to create your first product quickly. Here's the basic concept: Brainstorm a book or an e-book topic and write down the chapter titles. Then, write articles based on the topic of each chapter. When all of the articles are written, remove them from your web site and package them as a book. This is called re-purposing your intellectual property.

Re-Purpose Your Newsletter

You can use the same strategy with a newsletter. Each issue will become a chapter in your future book. Once all of the editions (future chapters) are complete, remove your newsletter archive from the web site and sell the book.

Create a Workbook

If you'd rather not write a lot, you can create a workbook with activities, templates, and exercises to help clients complete a task or achieve a goal.

Message Board "Hunt"

Message boards contain a wealth of information for a new product. Find online forums visited by your target audience and capture the most common questions asked. Answer each question in an article, which will later become a section or chapter in your book. You can also interview people who provide the most useful answers on the message boards and include them in your book or e-book.

First-Hand Research

First-hand research can be easily performed from your web site or by e-mail, helping you create a ready-to-sell product. One of my customers has a form on her web site, which asks visitors to submit their biggest challenge. She then gathers submissions and by addressing each challenge, assembles a great product. You can do the same by sending out an e-mail survey to your mailing list, asking them to tell you about their biggest problem.

Tape Your Coaching Sessions

When you coach a client, take notes or tape your sessions (with the client's permission). Everything you say when you coach is material original to you! Format your notes into a book, e-book, or workbook, depending on how your coaching sessions are structured.

You don't have to start with a full-blown book or e-book. You can start small, perhaps creating a checklist or questionnaire. Some coaches create tools they use with their own clients, and then offer them for sale on their web sites. You can later expand these tools into a full line of products–audio programs, books, workbooks, seminars, manuals-which then can be packaged together.

Even if you're a new coach, I can guarantee that you have something to teach others! Most people take their knowledge for granted. I remember a time when a financial planner visited me. As I was listening to him, I thought, "I wish I didn't have to understand all this stuff. This is all so confusing. Why can't I just tell him, 'Invest my money, and leave me alone! Why do I have to listen to all this jargon? Why?'" I felt I was really getting lost in the terminology he was using.

I realized that I'd completely spaced out and missed the last 10 minutes of his monologue. As he was about to leave, he asked, "So what are you up to these days?" I got excited, pulled out my CDs, and started telling him about my tele-conferences, audio products, new technology and web sites. He listened attentively for about five minutes, held the CDs in his hands, and said, "I guess this is how you feel when I talk finances."

We both took our knowledge for granted!

If you feel "ordinary"–lacking any special knowledge or expertise–let me share a unique strategy that works for many of my clients. It will get you on a roll with your first product in no time!

Dig for Gold in Your "Sent" Folder

Every day we send dozens of e-mails ... a piece of advice here, a checklist-on-the-fly there. Most of us routinely delete these diamonds in the rough without a second thought. Could these "sent" e-mails contain hidden product ideas, coaching tools, and other opportunities to generate additional revenue? Absolutely!

Many of the e-mails you write contain insights or advice in the area of your expertise. What if you could turn those one-time messages into "instant coaching tools," which others can use over and over again? Think of the possibilities! You could...

- Create a private client-only area so your clients could access your list of unique and original tools.

- Include the tools in a new client "Welcome Pack" to introduce them to your coaching process.

- Package your forms and documents into a product, and sell it on your web site.

- Supplement your collection of coaching tools with an audio CD, turning it into a comprehensive "coach-yourself" system.

- Print all the tools you create and arrange them in a binder to create a tangible, ready-to-sell product for your live events and expos.

I personally send at least 25 e-mails per day to customers, clients, prospects, and colleagues. Let's peek inside my "sent" folder.

Instant Coaching Tool #1. March 2: An e-mail on how to set up an "auto responder program" so it delivers PDF files automatically. Originally posted as a response to a discussion list question, this becomes a how-to checklist, *5 Steps to Delivering PDF Files via an Auto responder*.

Instant Coaching Tool #2. March 11: A message sent to a new client about the process of activating her web site, domain names, hosting accounts, DNS settings, etc. becomes *A Step-by-Step Timeline for Making Your Web Site Available Online*.

Instant Coaching Tool #3. November 12: A detailed message on the type of information to include on a coaching web site. Originally sent to a client suffering from "writer's block," this becomes *A Coaching Web Site Planning Workbook*. This is an actual product that I created a couple of years ago, which you can see in the book resources center.

Instant Coaching Tool #4. March 21: An inspirational e-mail written to a coach desperately seeking revenue ideas for her new business (she had no budget to hire a coach). This becomes a *Marketing Funnel Diagram for Coaches* tool.

As you can see, the possibilities are almost endless. Break out your pick and shovel and start looking for gold inside your "sent" folder! Look through your "sent" folder and copy anything that could be turned into a re-usable tool for coaching clients. Organize the information you find and turn each piece of information into a form, checklist, exercise, questionnaire, self-test, mini-report, how-to article, or any other format that makes sense.

If you do this once a month, I bet you'll come out with half a dozen new products a year!

Of course, quality is more important than quantity. Keep in mind that in addition to generating passive income, the goal of every product is to bring you clients. Many coaches sell products, but usually it's a one-time transaction. How do you convert a product buyer into a coaching client? That's what the next section is about.

The Ultimate Secret of Successful Products

The goal of your information products—books, e-books and audio programs—is not to only generate passive revenue. The ultimate goal is to get you the next sale—a participant in your coaching program, an order for a more expensive product, or a one-on-one coaching client.

Some of the most successful coaching products invite and inspire their readers or listeners to take the next step. This requires a special strategy—you need to plan your information product from the start and keep this goal in mind while creating it.

Over the years, I purchased hundreds of information products created by coaches and other experts. Through careful observation, I uncovered five secrets of coaching products that attract new clients.

Even some of the most successful coaches, authors, and business people aren't aware of these factors. Start using them in every product you develop from now on, and you'll be amazed at how much new business your products will generate for you!

Here they are:

**Five Secrets Of Designing Information Products
That Attract Coaching Clients**

1. You must <u>inspire</u> your reader through client stories and examples;

2. You must introduce your <u>unique process</u> or approach to solving their problem or achieving their goal;

3. You must make them think and <u>self-explore</u> through questions and self-assessments inside your product;

4. You must give them the <u>next step</u> for implementing what they learn in your product;

5. You must let your <u>personality</u> show through personal stories, examples, and beliefs.

Only if your product contains all five of these elements will it compel your readers to take the next step and hire you, or enroll into one of your coaching programs!

Starting a Subscription Web site

When most people think about a million dollars, they're in awe of the number. "How in the world can I make a million a dollars?" you might be thinking. "It's a lot of money."

True. But if you really think about it, it's just getting 300 customers to pay you $300 a month for one year…Or getting 400 customers to pay you $200 a month…Or getting 90 people to pay you $1,000 a month.

How can you make these kinds of numbers a reality? Certainly, one-on-one coaching will not get you there. The answer is – residual income via a subscription service.

Subscription web site creates predictable, monthly revenue that you can't get from individual coaching or selling products alone. A subscription service may be a membership web site, a coaching club, a continued education program, or anything else that fits your business model.

The beauty of running a membership-based web site is in the "back end"–the coaching clients you gain as a result. But, you must have a large mailing list or ways to tap into other people's networks to reach a lot of prospects in order to succeed with a subscription web site.

Below are two of the most lucrative subscription site models. Each one is centered on a different focal point. If you're looking for an additional source of revenue that doesn't require working additional hours for every new client, pay attention.

Membership Site Model #1: Training & Community

This model is based on self-education. It relies heavily on content but can be very lucrative when it comes to back-end sales. You can write articles, create tutorials, how-to articles, books, forms, assessments, and templates to share ideas for gaining a special skill or achieving a specific result. You can also conduct monthly training calls on various topics, invite guest trainers, and record each call. This is probably the most popular membership site model. Coachville has used this model for years and I used it for ACCPOW, as well.

Here are a few examples of Training & Community web sites created by coaches:

Stress-Free Community
Created by Denver Hudson
http://www.stressfreecommunity.com

This is a content-rich, coaching-based community that educates, inspires, and supports you in eliminating harmful stress, creating vibrant physical, mental, emotional and spiritual health; moving through midlife transitions, and learning skills that help you live your life more intentionally. Members receive personal attention and support from Life and Wellness Coach Denver Hudson.

Massage Business Center
Created by Elizabeth Fletcher Brown
http://www.massagebusinesscenter.com

This site provides massage therapists with business and marketing skills, inspirational success stories, as well as tools and resources to support them in creating prosperous massage businesses. The content includes teleclasses, workbooks, and a newsletter.

Membership Site Model #2: The Coaching Club

A coaching club is a community of peers in a specific niche market who come together for support and networking. The site can be used as a back-end program for seminar participants or as a supplement for individual coaching clients. It's the most lucrative subscription-coaching model of all. Ramon Williamson, one of the most successful coaches in the industry, has been leading coaching clubs since 1986. Here's what he said at the 1st ACCPOW Coaching Telesummit:

"A coaching club is a niche-specific membership program where participants gain access to a community of like-minded peers, content, models, tools, inspiration, and implementation support to advance their most important goals. Why do people join coaching clubs? For three main reasons:

1) Community: They want a place where they can meet others and talk shop.

2) Profound Knowledge: They want knowledge and inspiration, not just information, to shorten their timeline to success.

3) Save Time: They want a place where they can obtain instant, easy access to strategies, models, tools, and resources quickly."

To demonstrate how coaching clubs work, let me give you an example from how I structure my own coaching club. Every member of "Milana's Inner Circle" gets access to:

- Monthly Training Call (*on topics about business, marketing, entrepreneurship and coaching*)

- Full Subscription to the ACCPOW Coaching Business "Vault" (*article archive, teleseminars, tutorials, and my personal "rolodex" of resources!*)

- Monthly Mastermind Call (*60-Minute High-Level Mastermind Call, Including Q & A Discussion and Laser Group Coaching*)

- Access to all Recordings of Training and Mastermind Calls

- CDs, Transcripts, and Newsletter (*physically shipped to members monthly*)

- Free call-in days 4 times a year (*15-minute one-on-one calls*)

- Special treatment from Milana (*discounts, case studies, new strategies, tools, videos, and anything else I find absolutely key to share with my members!*)

I spend on average about 10 hours a month running "Milana's Inner Circle," including all calls, newsletter production, material preparation and answering questions on a private member-only forum. (You can learn more about my coaching club at www.milana.com/club)

The focal point of a coaching club is the peer-level mastermind process facilitated by the coach. Everyone brings their strategies, challenges, and success stories to the group. Everyone is a coach. It is the ultimate group-coaching environment!

In addition to providing group calls, you could create a password-protected area on your web site, where you would add:

- A discussion board (or discussion list)
- Links and resources pages
- Downloadable worksheets and checklists
- Recordings of the weekly coaching sessions

working" page, featuring your clients' names,
ound, and contact information

The best thing about the "coaching club" subscription model is that you simply facilitate and support the community you build. There's no pressure to produce fresh content every week. You are under no obligation to provide individual coaching or consulting to your members because the main benefit is networking with peers, and the growth opportunities this creates. You only have to coach two days a week, spending the rest of your time strategizing, planning and creating new ventures. Nothing can beat that!

The biggest distinction between a Coaching Club model and a Training and Community model is the pricing. The training & community model relies on the back-end sales (e.g. coaching programs, recommended products, and services, etc.). The pricing of this type of a subscription web site is therefore relatively low – $17 to $47 a month.

A coaching club is priced higher because it offers a more personalized approach and a higher level of access to you. You'll see coaching clubs priced anywhere between $97 and $497 a month. The "back-end" product of a coaching club model is high-priced 1-on-1 coaching offered to high level clients.

Which Membership Model is Right for You?

Where do you go from here? What's the best subscription model for your business? Consider these factors when making your decision:

➢ How much time can you invest in running your site?

> ➢ What is your desired outcome?

> ➢ What are your biggest strengths?

> ➢ What kinds of content or service can you offer?

> ➢ Who on your team can handle the day-to-day tasks?

> ➢ What is your ultimate purpose for a membership site?

Each model requires a different set of answers to these questions so be sure to think about these before making a decision.

A final comment on membership web sites: Many coaches make a mistake of creating a ton of content, then wonder why their retention rate is so low. People join, download everything they're interested in, and cancel their membership. This is true for all membership-based web sites, not just in coaching.

So how do you keep members subscribed and add new members all the time? The secret is in focusing on people, not on content. Mastermind groups, group coaching calls, mentor sessions, question and answer calls, "buddy" circles, and other peer-based groups are what will keep your members excited!

Part V: In a Nutshell

1. When one-on-one coaching is your only source of income, it will always be limited to the number of hours you're able and willing to work. You must create passive income sources on a regular basis and become not only better off financially, but have a lot more freedom with your time, as well.

2. There are three types of passive coaching income: truly passive, leveraged, and residual, which offer the highest potential income source of all.

3. You can create your first product from existing materials - articles, teleseminars, e-mails, presentations or anything else you developed over the years.

4. One of the best ways to build a long-lasting business and enjoy residual income is to start a subscription web site. There are three lucrative subscription site models: coaching clubs, group coaching, and training & community. The model you choose should depend on your lifestyle, preferences, and long-term goals.

Part VI
Creating a Self-Propelled
Lifestyle Business

"Whenever you see a successful business, someone once made a courageous decision"
— Peter F. Drucker

Building a Business that Works Without You

Five years ago, I took a weeklong vacation in Wildwood, New Jersey–a small and quiet family resort that we'd visited three summers in a row. Maybe it's the Fudge Kitchen on the boardwalk that kept us coming back, but we couldn't find another destination that was so close and family-friendly.

Before each vacation, I would worry about who would take care of my business. I was receiving 200 to 500 e-mails a day, and knew that my Internet provider's mail server couldn't store thousands of e-mails until my return. So, before our first trip to Wildwood, I left my computer on with my e-mail program open, hoping it would automatically check for new messages every few minutes and empty the mail server.

When I returned from vacation, I saw that my anti-virus program had blocked one suspicious message. After that, my program stopped checking for new messages. Half of all the messages were returned to senders, leaving me with a customer support disaster.

In the years after this incident, I looked for solutions to this problem–auto responders, message forwarding, even checking my e-mail at a local library where I was vacationing. Finally, I realized that the only efficient solution was to have someone check my e-mail for me. A month before my vacation in 2002, I hired a temporary assistant. For one week only, she would check my messages and reply to customers as needed.

This gave me peace of mind, and even allowed me to vacation for more than one week. Then I thought, "If my assistant can take care of my e-mail, what else can I delegate to her or to others that will free me up for something more productive on a permanent basis?" I wrote down every task involved in running my business, and ended up with a long list: instant proof that I wasn't just playing solitaire on the computer all day long.

I instantly saw that all the items under administrative tasks could be delegated to others. I hired an accountant and an administrative assistant, and instantly added five more hours a week for revenue-generating activities, business planning, or just taking a nap in the middle of the day.

You must think of your business differently.

"Pretend that the business you own is the prototype, or will be the prototype, for 5,000 more just like it. Not almost like it, but just like it. Perfect replicates, clones." This is what Michael E. Gerber wrote in *The E-Myth* about building a business that can function perfectly without your physical presence. Of course, if you're a coach, and coaching is all you do, then replicating your practice 5,000 times would be impossible. There is only one person who can coach like you: YOU.

If you develop new ways to generate income–workshops, products, programs, licensing, and training–then you can create a business that almost runs itself! Andrea J. Lee, the author of *Multiple Streams of Coaching Income*, offers several thought-provoking questions to help you get there:

> "Think of your business as anything but a job! Go to work ON your business rather than IN it, and ask yourself the following questions:
>
> - How can I get my business to work, but without me?
> - How can I get my people to work, but without my constant interference?
> - How can I own my business, and still be free of it?
> - How can I spend my time doing the work I love to do rather than the work I have to do?"
>
> - *Andrea J. Lee, Multiple Streams of Coaching Income*

The only way to accomplish this is to have a *documented process*–your own Business Operations Manual. Without such a manual, your business approach will be less disciplined and more difficult to automate.

One of my favorite movies is *Executive Decision.* There is a scene where Kurt Russell has to fly a large plane after receiving just a few previous flight lessons. The first thing he asks the flight attendant, played by Halle Berry, is something like: "Quick! Hand me that Flight Manual! Now, find the section on standard landing procedures! Quick, before we crash!"

This is an extreme analogy, but still appropriate. Personally, I can no longer imagine operating my business without my "flight manual"–my Business Operations Manual.

So, if you feel like you're living in the same "rat race" you once experienced as an employee, it's time to do something about it!

The key to working fewer hours is leveraging everything you do and creating passive revenue sources from products (e-books, audio programs, manuals, private web sites, books) and services that generate large amounts of money in a single shot (seminars, teleseminars, and workshops). You'll be able to earn money without continuously working for it. You will create something once, and let it earn money for you for many years to come.

Another key to creating a self-propelled business is being completely focused on, and dedicated to, living your dream lifestyle. It drives me crazy when people say, "I wish I lived in a..." or "I would love to go to…" and never do these things. Why not? It's your life! You can make it happen! Snap your fingers and say, "I can make my business work without me!"

Let's keep the momentum going and talk about how you can accomplish this.

Painting Yourself Into a Corner

How do most coaches start their business? They do everything themselves. In trying to save some money, they spend 50% to 80% of their time working *"in"* their businesses: coaching clients, editing articles, handling support requests, and doing their own accounting. In other words, they place themselves so deep into the operation and administration of their business that they feel like it cannot run without them.

If you're lucky, you'll realize sooner rather than later that it's time to start delegating–time to let others free up your time so you can focus on doing what only you can do.

Successful coaches invest 80% of their time working "on" their businesses: developing new programs, creating new products, building new strategic alliances, and coaching high-end clients and groups.

Are you working ON your business or just IN it?

During a practice management-coaching program I was a part of, I heard one participant say that her business tripled after she started delegating. That sounded very strange to me. Hire people; pay them money out of your own pocket, and your income triples? How's that possible? Mulling this over, I decided to examine the way I was doing business.

I revisited the list of all of my business-related activities I created earlier, and split it into three columns to create a table I call my "Activity Grid."

Things that only I can do, and enjoy doing them	Things I can do myself, but could easily be done by someone else	Things I don't know how to do and don't want to learn them
Coaching & Consulting Marketing & Writing Research & Education Strategizing & Development Product Development Advanced Web Site Development Conducting Teleclasses Speaking E-mail Correspondence Copywriting Networking	Basic Web Design Graphic Design Research & Information Gathering Article Submission Newsletter Publishing Membership Site Administration Computer Programming Copywriting Office Organizing Customer Service Issuing Refunds Shipping Products Prospect Follow-up Designing Presentations Recording Teleclasses	Accounting & Bookkeeping Office Maintenance Software Development Transcription
	Need to Delegate	**Need to Delegate**

Figure 1: My Personal Activity Grid

After creating this grid, I stared at it for a while. The right-hand column was easy–I knew I needed an accountant, a computer expert and a transcriber. But one nagging question kept surfacing about the middle column: "Who could possibly do ALL of these things, and do them as well as I?"

As it turned out, I found that person within just a few days, and she could do it all BETTER and FASTER than me.

Virtual Assistant: A Coach's Best Friend

If I could give just one piece of advice to a new coach, it would be this: hire a virtual assistant (VA) as soon as possible. Find a way to pay her, even if you can afford only five hours a month. Consider this a *must* for operating your business, just like investing in a computer, a phone line or business cards.

What's a virtual assistant?

Through the Internet, e-mail, fax and phone, the VA communicates with, and provides services to, small businesses, entrepreneurs, and individuals who need administrative support but don't want to hire an employee, purchase equipment or manage an office. The tasks performed by a VA will largely depend on her background and skills, and your requirements.

If your VA doesn't possess *all* of the skills needed for every project, she will outsource particular activities. For example, your VA might be an excellent copywriter, but have zero experience designing web sites. In that case, she'll subcontract with a third-party web designer. If one of your primary tasks is invoicing and updating financial data, you might want a VA specializing in those tasks, but one who can perform general administrative work as well.

Whether you require expertise in accounting, bookkeeping, document processing, data management, coaching support, small business support, research, mailing, web design, or just some assistance sending out personal invitations, a VA can help. A good VA will have a strong background in computers and the Internet—usually learned from prior experience in a corporate setting.

Because a VA partnership is based on trust, it's important to feel comfortable with the person you select. You must work to win her trust just as she must work to win yours. Once mutual trust has been established, it's easier to delegate responsibilities with minimal oversight and review. Since a VA is a professional who works alone, you and your VA should agree on the number of hours she'll work each week or month, and agree on compensation.

Beyond feeling that "no one can do this better than me," the most difficult thing about the process of hiring a VA was accepting that I would have to outsource things I could do myself. At first, I felt that I'd be throwing money away, but nothing was further from the truth. Delegating freed me to focus on the most important things in my business: creating and implementing growth strategies through alliances, product development, and promotion. Delegating has improved my business operations, income, and quality of life.

Today, my "dream team" consists of:

-   A **Virtual Assistant** to handle all administrative tasks, such as customer service, web site updates, newsletter publishing, and other urgent issues, which would distract me from my primary business operations. I have recently added a second virtual assistant to my business, so that, if one is overloaded with work or away on vacation, she can easily transfer all the tasks to the second one.

-   **A Membership Coordinator** to run and manage my coaching club.

-   **An Accountant** to handle my receipts, bills, taxes, reconciling, bank transactions, etc.

-   **An Administrative Assistant** for office organizing, filing, packing, labeling, and shipping products to customers.

-   **A Computer Technician** for troubleshooting and maintaining my home network, printers, back-up systems and basically keeping me safe from panic attacks!

- **A Graphic Designer** to create logos, brochures, CD inserts and labels, and anything else that requires a professional look.

- **A Transcriptionist** to transcribe all my tele-seminars, interviews and training calls I conduct.

I'm pleased to report that my "yuck bucket" is almost always empty, and I spend MUCH MORE time focusing on the activities at which I excel and that I truly enjoy.

So, what did I learn from creating my personal activity grid?

Bottom line: delegating is a critical factor for success. Even though just a year ago, it seemed outrageous to hire someone else to do the work I usually do—today, I can't imagine running my business without my team! If you're having a problem finding a good assistant, e-mail me. I have a program called "Send Your VA to School" (www.sendyourVAtoschool.com), and keep track of all the virtual assistants who go through it.

A friend once told me, "You can't afford to major in minors!" In other words, if you spread your focus by taking care of the "little" things in your business, you won't be able to get really good at the things that really matter.

Don't be afraid to *trust* others with your business tasks. Create your own Activity Grid and think about what you should be doing yourself and what you should be delegating to others. It's an amazing feeling to wake up every day knowing that someone else will take care of the things that drive you crazy, while you'll do only the things you truly enjoy.

Making the Most Out of Your Time

The most frequent question I get from clients and colleagues is this: "Milana, you have a few dozen web sites, five subscription services, coaching clients, and two small children. How are you able to accomplish so much in just a few hours a day?"

"I have a secret," I say. "I have no other choice!"

The truth is, the only time I'm able to work is when my children are either asleep or at school. That amounts to about 5 hours each day, considering that I take an hour-long lunch and a morning walk.

Since starting my company, I've been trying to perfect my schedule. I went from working three hours a day, to 10 hours a day, and then back to five hours. During this "roller coaster" ride, I learned one thing: regardless of how much time you devote to your business–three hours or 10 hours–it's what you do with that time that counts.

Most people work full-time jobs to earn a living. They must be physically present for six to eight hours a day regardless of how many hours it actually takes for them to complete their daily tasks.

After years of running my business, I learned that it's NOT about working a set number of hours or days each week. It's about achieving your *desired result,* no matter how much or how little time it takes. One phone call can create a new income source for the next 12 months or more. A single connection can result in a highly profitable joint venture.

These concepts are the fuel for continual debates within my family. My husband, who works in the medical field, doesn't "get" my work schedule. Coming home after eight hours of hospital work, he wonders how my business produces any income when I work only a couple of hours a day (6 hours on my busiest days).

When I first quit my job, my daughter was just a toddler and I felt like I never had enough time to do anything! Within a few months, however, I learned how to condense my eight-hour workload into a four-hour day. More importantly, I came to understand that it doesn't matter how many hours I work. Sometimes I work for just 15 minutes a day and feel incredibly productive!

What I'm about to share with you may sound surprising–even shocking. But please bear with me and keep an open mind. After working with many frustrated and very busy coaches, I have come up with an approximate number of hours each strategy below will save you. These timesaving strategies have worked wonders for me personally! Pay special attention if you stay home with your children. This may be the answer to your prayers.

For example, only go to the networking events where you are in the spotlight. If you attend a networking meeting and you are not a presenter, make sure it's a highly targeted group of people who need your solutions. Write down every organization you belong to, and ask yourself these three questions:

- What are the chances of meeting someone who needs my services?
- What are the chances of meeting someone who knows someone who needs my services?
- If I give a presentation to these people, how many would be interested in what I have to say?

Don't network for the sake of networking. C.J. Hayden, the author of "Get Clients Now," refers to this behavior as "networking addiction." When you go out to network, make sure it's the best use of your time, every time! (By the way, driving to and from these events also counts as your work time!)

Another way you can save a lot of time is keeping track of all of your business-related information in one place. This may include:

- Account user names and passwords
- List of vendors and resources
- Partners' and assistants' contact information
- Software pass codes
- Weekly schedule of activities

This should be a file you can give to an assistant or family member whenever you're unable to take care of your business.

Automate your follow-up as much as possible. I'm amazed to see how many coaches send follow-up letters manually. With auto responder services becoming so easy to use and affordable, there's no reason not to automate your messages.

Do you send your clients invoices? This means that you are not only asking them to make a purchase decision every month, but you also have to process their payments manually. What a hassle! Use a recurring billing option through your merchant account or shopping cart to automate this process.

Anyone who has more than 10 one-on-one coaching clients is either overwhelmed or has very little time to work ON their business. I highly recommend that you limit the number of clients you work with at any given time. Taking on too many clients is the #1 reason that coaches become overwhelmed and burned out. Decide how many hours a week you want to work and divide this figure by three. That's the maximum number of clients you should take. For example, if you want to work 30 hours a week, you should have no more than 10 coaching clients. The other 20 hours should be spent on marketing and creative work.

Finally, I'd like to share a very important strategy with you. This strategy will stretch your thinking and make you go outside your comfort zone for just a few moments.

The Most Productive 15 Minutes a Day

Think about what you can do in 15 minutes that will be more productive than a full day's work? There are certain things you can do in 15 minutes that will keep paying you for months or even years!

Here are some ideas:

- Call a potential joint venture partner to discuss cross-promotion or a new product idea.

- Submit your article to hundreds of directories and newsletter publishers.

- Create an overview of your new book, teleclass, workshop, or any other product.

- Set up an auto responder to follow up with coaching prospects, newsletter subscribers, Teleclass participants, or customers.

Ask yourself every day: "What is the best use of my time, right now?" Eliminate activities that drain time and resources but don't help you meet your goals. This will help you cut your working time by at least 5-10 hours a week!

Many people don't appreciate the gift of time. Whenever I see store clerks or customer service reps with nothing to do, I wonder what they're thinking. There they are, in the middle of the day, with no customers. They just sit "twiddling their thumbs." Can you imagine how much they could achieve during this "down time?" Provided their manager allowed them, they could be...

- Exploring a new profession
- Learning a new skill
- Catching up on their mail
- Writing a book
- Doing research
- Listening to seminar tapes

When I worked as a telemarketer during my first years in America, I was able to read, write computer programs, and finish all of my college homework. Talk about leveraging time... ALL the time!

What are you doing with your time when you're waiting in line, stuck in traffic, or waiting at your child's swimming classes? I write some of my best articles and come with some of my most exciting ideas while waiting for my kids at their karate classes.

How to Start Your Own Coaching Team

So far, I've talked about leveraging passive income and automating your coaching business. But there's another way to create a business that works without you–building a team of coaches. Many successful coaches have recruited other coaches for their businesses. They've done this for different reasons, which include:

- Adding value for clients by providing coaching in other areas.
- Sharing the workload of developing and running coaching programs.
- Implementing action plans they've designed with clients.
- Acquiring a mastermind partner.
- Increasing visibility in their field.
- Handling overflows of clients.
- Creating a coaching company they can sell in the future.

Launching a coaching team doesn't have to be an elaborate process. It can be as simple as examining your network of clients, customers and participants, and asking these questions:

- Who is savvy and familiar enough with my methods?
- Who shares my beliefs and goals?
- Who do I enjoy working with the most?
- Who has the potential to be a great partner?
- Who'd be excited to work with me, side-by-side?
- Who has skills and abilities that I lack?

Once you've answered these questions, invite the best candidate(s) to join your team.

Before you dive in, however, there are certain steps you must follow to ensure the success of your coaching team:

1. ***Create a system or document a process.*** When a coach joins your team, she wants a system she can follow. She wants a proven process she can walk clients through–a ready-to-use "operations manual." Create a step-by-step coaching process you'd like team members to use with clients *before* you hire another coach.

2. ***Decide how to train team members.*** Hopefully, you'll have a "pool" of fans–customers and clients who are already familiar with your methods and philosophies. To make training even more effortless, record everything you do–teleseminars, live events, workshops, etc. That way, you can simply hand your team members written and/or recorded materials for them to study. If you'd like, you can also charge them while you train them. Make sure they regularly attend your live events and programs to speed the training process.

3. ***Establish the roles you and your team members will play.*** Determine, in advance, which roles your new team member will play. He can be a facilitator, implementation coach, workshop leader, assistant, or fill any other position you have. It's important that both of you understand the nature of your relationship and responsibilities. This will become even clearer as you identify your overall business goals and determine how your coaching team fits into the big picture.

4. ***Develop up a mutually beneficial pricing structure.*** You want to reward your coaches according to their experience. Some coaching team leaders pay $100 - $200 an hour, on a percentage basis, or even on a no-fee basis. Your pricing structure will be shaped by what you and your associate coaches want from the relationship.

5. ***Determine which qualifications you need.*** Create an ideal profile of the people you want on your team. Remember, you're not looking for another "you." You're looking for someone to *complement* your unique abilities and talents. That's how you can build a truly great coaching team.

I have recently added a coach to my team for the first time. It was an eye-opening experience because I had to let go of many reasons and excuses for not doing it. Finally, I put together a list of all the things I am looking for in a coach to join me, and sent it to a few people I thought might be interested. One person responded within a couple of hours. She turned out to be the best thing that ever happened to me.

The most important decision I had to make before bringing another coach into my business was to decide her role. I didn't want a clone of me, but I needed someone savvy enough to grasp the process I teach. I also wanted someone passionate about my mission.

There are many ways to build and run your coaching team. Every coach I interviewed about this topic has been using a different team model (see www.buildacoachingteam.com for details). Regardless of how your coaching team looks, it will allow you to take your business to a whole new level of operation.

Here are some questions for you to think about:

- How would your business look if you added another coach?

- What would his or her role be in your business?

- What would your role be?

Part VI: In a Nutshell

1. If your income depends on how many hours you work, then you don't have a business, you have a practice. A business must generate revenue from two or more sources–products, events, alliances, workshops, etc.–with clients representing just one of the revenue streams.

2. When developing your business, you must look at it as the prototype for 5,000 more businesses just like it. This will lead you to create systems, processes, and a team that can take care of these processes without you being in the business.

3. Don't paint yourself into a corner. Determine what you do best, and then delegate everything else. Hire a virtual assistant (VA) as soon as you possibly can, even if for just a few hours a month. This will help you to empty your "yuck bucket" on a regular basis and truly enjoy your business.

4. There are 9 different ways you can make the most of your time, and have at least 25% more free time every week. Productivity does not equal time - your most productive activity may take as little as 15 minutes a day and pay you for years to come.

5. A great way to leverage your time, earn passive income, and build a solid company is to create your own team of coaches. There are 5 elements you need to have in place to bring a coach into your business: systems, training, assigned functions, pricing structure, and personal qualifications.

Part VII
Leadership, Edge and
Innovation

"Two roads diverged in a wood, and I, I took the one less traveled by, and that has made all the difference."
— Robert Frost

Be a Legend in Your Own Mind

I recently took my daughter to her friend's birthday party at a local bowling alley. One of the girls was wearing a t-shirt that read, "I am a legend in my own mind." That made me think: how many people in the world can say these words and actually mean them? How many people believe that they are unique, one of a kind, a legend?

Many coaches try to hide behind their company names, thinking it's unethical to "toot their own horn." Some of the biggest, most successful organizations have been built under their owners' names!

Donald Trump was originally going to call his Trump Tower by another name—Tiffany Tower. That's because the famous jewelry store was right next door. When he asked a friend about which name is better—Trump Tower or Tiffany Tower—the friend said, "When you change your name to Tiffany, call it Tiffany Tower."

I am not going to bore you with another rant on leadership. But I will tell you that in a market full of "look-alikes," the only way to be perceived as the best is to BE the best. Stand out, take a position, innovate, and stay on the leading edge in your field.

What does it really take to be innovative?

You must think the unthinkable. Do what's never been done before. Until I created the Coaching Telesummit, this concept simply didn't exist. Sure, people held teleseminars, invited guest speakers, and brought large audiences together over a conference line. Nobody had ever created a highly niched, weeklong tele-event with panel discussions and "hot seats" that hundreds of people were willing to pay $200-$500 each to attend.

When I asked several experts in my field if they think this telesummit is a good idea, they told me, "No way that anybody is going to spend 3 hours on the phone 8 days in a row! You'll have to pay THEM to come!" Now, after people saw how successful and lucrative it can be (I generated six figures and opened many new doors each year I held it), similar "telesummits" pop up in every possible industry!

Before I developed the Assessment Generator, coaches were offering their assessment forms in static downloadable format (Word or PDF). It was impossible to capture a client lead when there was no way to automate their assessments. I thought, wouldn't it be great to create a tool that can automatically "spit out" scoring results, while capturing a new client lead! When I shared the idea with my mentors, they told me it might be a waste of time: it's too technical, it's too complicated, and nobody will get the concept.

I went ahead anyway, because I knew it would solve my own problem of generating leads. It did, and today every other coaching web site I visit has an automated self-scoring assessment, even if they're using their own custom solution.

I am not saying this to brag (although I AM extremely proud of pioneering these concepts). But I share this with you to demonstrate how following your "gut feeling" and doing what nobody has ever done before can take you into a brave new realm as being an innovator and a leader in your market.

So what are some of the ways that you could become the #1 coach in your niche? How could you position yourself so that you and your company are top of mind when people think of your specialty? What does it take for a prospective client to say, "I don't want someone *like* her, I want *HER*?"

Here are just a few ideas followed by real-life examples of how other coaches use innovative strategies to build a strong position in their niche:

Ways to Position Yourself as the Leading Coach in Your Niche

- Start an association
- Open a training school
- Conduct industry-wide surveys
- Partner with "movers and shakers" in your field
- Develop a licensing program
- Create an annual industry-wide event
- Start a directory of providers or resources within your niche
- Solve problem for your target audience

When I talk to coaches about creating a product or program, I usually hear this: "There are so many people who know this stuff, why do you think anybody will want to buy it from me?" The question you should be asking yourself is, why *not* you? Sure, many people know this stuff, but *you* will be the one taking action on it!

Anyone could've held a teleconference on coaching future predictions, but I was the one who took this concept and ran with it! Over six hundred people came to listen to some of the top experts on coaching, and we recorded almost three hours worth of amazing ideas, conversations, and predictions!

Creativity and innovation is the key to becoming a true leader in your industry. Innovation *is* leadership. Coaches are a highly creative "breed," which you will see it in just a moment.

Innovation in Action

I truly believe that innovation is inspired by observation and keeping yourself in that "anything-is-possible!" state of mind. Some days, I 'm really on a roll with new ideas. Those days usually happen after I read a new book, attend an event, or do research.

To help you become more creative in thinking about your business, I am including some of the most unique and innovative ideas and concepts I found in the coaching world. Each of the following examples of innovation began when a coach identified a need among a particular group of people. Read, observe, and then brainstorm about how to fill a need in YOUR niche.

Accelerated Home-Study Training Course for Coaches
www.coachtrainingaccelerator.com

Many would-be coaches are intimidated by the extensive training and large financial investment required. That's why Will Craig, founder of the Coach Training Alliance, created a 20-week self-placed, home study program, which basically provides a blueprint that new coaches can use at a fraction of the usual costs. The Coach Training Accelerator includes the Coach Training Course, Client Tools, and Resource Library. (These resources can even help established coaches to quickly build a successful practice.) As an alternative, coaches may also choose a 22-week comprehensive live training program where they can use the Coach Training Accelerator in combination with group mentoring and real-time coaching practice, and receive feedback from experienced Master coaches.

International Association of Career Coaches
www.iaccweb.org

Marcia Bench is a career coach, author of 18 books and the founder of the Career Coach Institute. As a pioneer in the emerging field of career coaching, she saw the need for a worldwide association designed specifically for coaches specializing in career development. Member benefits include access to an online community of career professionals, coaching and job search tools, as well as insurance, Teleclass bridge lines, and mentoring opportunities.

Coaching For Every Budget - The Money Gym
www.themoneygym.com

Nicola Cairncross started an online community, which is a combination of a "coaching gym" and "coaching club." It is innovative because of the choices offered to customers of all budgets and needs. She has four levels of membership–Silver, Gold and Platinum Memberships and the Full Coaching program. Obviously, clients receive more products, services, and personal attention when they choose the pricier packages.

Worldwide Parent-Teen Learning Circles
www.compassionateparenting.com

Dr. Beth is giving parent coaching a big spin! Why coach dozens or hundreds of parents when you can coach thousands (even millions) worldwide by encouraging schools, churches and youth groups to promote your parent-teen conferences, learning circles and facilitators? That's exactly what Dr. Beth has done with her Compassionate Parenting worldwide teleconferences and support groups. Her National Teleconference Series brings thousands of parents and teens together to listen to each other's concerns, get answers to their questions and receive valuable information about how they can navigate and actually enjoy the teen years.

Coaching "Reality Show"
www.AttractionMarketing.com

Would you like to generate major publicity for your coaching business for almost six months-absolutely FREE? That's exactly what Wanda Loskot did by creating, hosting and facilitating an online 20-week coaching "reality show", similar to Donald Trump's *The Apprentice*. The results: a ready-to-publish book, thousands of people in the audience watching the "show," and a loyal base of clients for years to come. She first screened applicants by asking them a few questions, after which she chose the finalists, and gave them weekly challenges related to their businesses. Meanwhile, the audience (people from Wanda's mailing list) watched, commented, and voted for their favorite participant. The winner qualified to receive a full year of one-on-one coaching with Wanda.

Information Product Factory
www.90dayproduct.com

A 90-day intensive group program designed for coaches, consultants, speakers, and information entrepreneurs who want to create a product fast. Most people procrastinate and wallow in doubt when it comes to creating products. Michael Port and Mitch Meyerson offer a program that gives participants knowledge, tools, and "forces" new authors to stay on track to complete their product in three months.

International Relationship Coaching Training Organization
www.relationshipcoachinginstitute.com

David Steele is founder and CEO of the Relationship Coaching Institute, and has trained over 5,000 professionals in his methods of relationship coaching. With 20+ years of experience in family and marriage therapy, David saw a need to help professionals understand how successful relationships work and how to help couples and singles live joyful lives. His Relationship Coaching Institute offers training programs, certifications, seminars, and an active, membership-based community of relationship coaches.

Send Your Virtual Assistant to School
www.sendyourVAtoschool.com

For months my clients and coaching club members have been telling me they need a good VA. There are many VA training schools who teach them the basics of administrative support, but that was not enough for coaching entrepreneurs. Finally, I decided to do something about it. I developed a 3-day accelerated program specifically for the virtual assistants who work (or want to work) with coaches. I personally trained them in the marketing strategies and the tools they would need to use to support their clients on a much higher level. I also invited my own virtual assistants and asked them to share their best tips and resources. Now any time I have a client or a member who needs their VA to "upgrade" their skills, I simply send them this training program. I solved a problem for my clients and for myself, while developing a new product I can sell over and over again.

How to Come Up with Big Innovative Ideas

I truly believe that innovation is *not* something you're born with. It is something you develop and nurture over time. Being innovative is like a muscle that needs exercise to be strong. Here are my personal strategies for constantly being on the leading edge in business:

Ten Ways to Be Innovative and Stay on the Leading Edge in Your Industry

1. Create space and time on a weekly basis to brainstorm and strategize.
2. Survey your target audience to understand the needs of your market.
3. Tap into your deep desire to find solutions to their challenges.
4. Never overload yourself with clients.
5. Take time away from the business.
6. Read industry publications to spot trends, needs, and wants.
7. Accept risk and the possibility of failure.
8. Create a time without distractions.
9. Remember that innovation does not respond to pressure.
10. Attend a mastermind group on a regular basis.

Let me stop here for just a moment. I think being a part of a mastermind group is so important that it deserves a few more words.

What do the most brilliant people in the world do to achieve far more in less time? They get together to brainstorm. They think "outside the box." They strategize. They "mastermind!"

In a "mastermind" environment, where nobody is holding back and everyone has a strong desire to help, breakthroughs often happen! Big decisions are made, joint ventures are created, and life-long friendships are formed.

There are a few important considerations you need to make before starting your own mastermind group:

Questions to Ask Yourself Before Starting a Mastermind Group

- Who will you invite to your group and how will you do it?

- How can you make sure that everyone gets the most out of your meetings?

- How do you deal with confidentiality and competition in the group?

- How can you solve any conflicts that may arise?

- How do you keep your group energized and productive for months or years?

- How do you structure your meetings so that all members look forward to them every time?

In my experience, the most critical consideration is inviting the RIGHT people to join your group! Everything else will fall into place.

What kind of people would you like to get feedback from? What kind of people would like to receive feedback from you? Who would you absolutely love to brainstorm with on a regular basis? These are some questions you want to ask yourself before starting your own mastermind group.

Another strategy for creating innovative ideas is based on momentum. This strategy has propelled me farther than any other.

Taking advantage of being excited by an idea, a concept, a book, an event, or a person, and then moving on it *while* I'm still in that state of mind, really works! I've seen this dozens of times. I'll sign up for a seminar with a couple of buddies or get the same e-book as them and the next day, I develop a new strategy or a product idea while they just file the materials away.

To take any kind of action, it's crucial that I be excited–in the "moment." It sometimes interferes with setting priorities, but that's how I've been able to launch many successful products and ideas.

Since my business expanded, I've had to modify my "now-or-never" approach. Today, when I get an idea, I give it 72 hours. If I'm still as excited three days later, I begin working on it. Many times, I'll go to sleep excited about something, only to wake up realizing that it wasn't as good as I thought. Or I'll realize that it was much more complicated than it first appeared. If I wait a few days, and the idea is still as appealing as when I first thought of it, I go for it!

I've dropped many projects this way, and moved on to bigger things–things that were (perhaps) easier to implement or had a bigger payoff.

Obsessing over something helps me bring that idea to fruition. In college, I always worked hard and stayed committed to every class. In fact, I became so fascinated about each subject that I considered majoring in every one of them! My astronomy professor looked at me in great surprise when I asked, "What do you have to major in to become an astronomer?" My interest quickly subsided, however, when she answered, "Physics."

Lessons My Coach Taught Me

I consider my coach to be one of the brightest minds in the business world. There is probably no product he hasn't tried, book he hasn't read, seminar he hasn't attended, or business leader he hasn't met.

What my coach doesn't know is that when I first hired him, my plan was to squeeze the best "juice" out of him, get his best ideas, then let him go after about 3-4 months. His monthly fee was higher than my mortgage, so I knew I couldn't keep him around much longer.

It is now three years later, and I am still his client. He works with very few people, charges a lot of money, and prefers to work behind the scenes of his clients' success. His wisdom is priceless and any week that passes without talking to him seems like a year.

During countless hours of conversations, there have been certain themes, concepts, and ideas that have surfaced again and again. I want to share them with you here. The conversation about being on the leading edge simply wouldn't be complete without them. They've completely changed the way I think and do business now.

1. Only implement product ideas that have a high-ticket or recurring-income back-end product ideas (e.g. an e-book channels readers into a coaching program on the back end; a live workshop channels participants into a year-long coaching "gym").

2. When you have dozens of new ideas, implement only the ones that fit into the bigger picture of your business.

3. Always have a big picture for your business. It's the only way to achieve consistent growth and peace of mind.

4. There is enough information in the world. What people need is implementation guidance and support. (That's why I created Milana's Inner Circle–most coaches know what they need to do, but either don't know how or lack guidance and support).

5. Identify what you're best at and do only those things. Delegate, outsource, automate, or eliminate the rest.

6. There are only three things people want to know before hiring you as a coach: 1) Do you understand my problem? 2) Have you ever helped people with this problem? 3) Can you help someone like me?

7. Don't push for sales. Instead, overwhelm people with value and allow them to buy. *Believe* in the value of your products. Everyone who should have them will buy them.

8. Be more experimental and try more things than your clients. That's what's really going to make you valuable to them.

9. The best things in business are *not* free. You have to pay to get the best information, the best advice, and the best strategies.

10. Always think outside the box. There is no right or wrong answer. There is a tested and proven answer.

Part VII: In a Nutshell

1. Innovation is not something you're born with. Like a muscle, it needs to be developed and nurtured over time. Use my strategies or find your own ways of being on the edge of innovation in your industry.

2. A mastermind group is a must for any business owner and entrepreneur. In a "mastermind" environment, where nobody is holding back and everyone has a strong desire to help, breakthroughs often happen! Big decisions are made, joint ventures are created, and great friendships are formed that will last a lifetime.

Part VIII
Shortening and Accelerating Your Path to Success

"We can learn from our mistakes, but it's better to learn from our successes."
— Donald Trump

An Easier Road to Riches

I wake up every morning feeling blessed. Although I'm not a deeply religious person, I thank God for giving me the opportunities and resources not to worry about food, shelter, paying bills, or losing my job.

Life hasn't always been this comfortable. I remember how frightened I was first coming to America 15 years ago. Having no command of spoken English and having been trained in a profession that held no prospects, I was sure I'd have to spend my life working as a dishwasher or a nanny, like many Russian women do.

I also remember how foolish I felt after quitting a perfectly good job to stay home with my second child. At the time, I had only one client and, with my husband still in school, I had no idea how we'd survive. I wish I could go back in time and tell my younger self, "Everything will be OK. Just keep doing what you're doing, and you'll be successful beyond your imagination."

If I could talk to myself 15 years ago, I would have shortened my path to success by at least five or seven years! There are so many things I wish I'd known...so many mistakes I could've avoided.

In fact, as someone who's absolutely fascinated with the idea of time travel, I would love to write my younger self a letter. It's a very personal letter, but what the heck!

Milana's Letter

Dear Milana,

First, I know how you feel–calm down. Everything will be OK. Everything will fall into place, and life will soon be much easier.

Second, stop taking music classes. You have taken enough! Yes, I know you've spent your whole life studying to be a music teacher but it's just not in the cards. You love music but you hate giving private lessons. You'll discover this very soon, so let me save you some time: call the parents of your students and tell them you're quitting. Their children will be thrilled.

Now, what you need to do is learn how to use a computer. Take classes at a local college (no, not computer programming– you'll hate that too). Take basic computer classes, enough to learn how to type fast and become an expert word processor. Then, enroll as a business major. Pay attention in Marketing 101! You'll be glad you did.

When a friend tells you about a new Internet class forming in the summer, RUN to sign up! It's only one credit, but it will change your life. I know the instructor looks weird, but don't look at him– look at your screen.

You'll get many job offers as you approach graduation, but tell them to leave you alone–you've got better plans. Here's what I want you to do. Go on the Internet and find a copy of Ken Evoy's *Make Your Knowledge Sell*. Get it, read it, memorize it. It will teach you everything you need to know about creating information products from scratch. I realize you haven't read a single book in English yet (aside from college textbooks), but don't worry–it's completely practical and a great read! You'll love it!

Okay, here is where I want you to listen very carefully. Don't write a book about Web design. Don't create the "Helping Foot" web site–it might be cute, but it will distract you from the real business you'll be starting.

Instead, go to Coachville.com and become a member. Visit Teleclass.com and sign up for every teleclass on coaching, business, or marketing you can find. Harv Eker's *Secrets of the Millionaire Mind* won't be published for another few years, but get a copy of his *Speedwealth–How to Make a Million in Your Own Business in 3 Years or Less.* It's the next best thing!

While you're at it, grab a copy of Michael Gerber's *The E-Myth*–you might not understand it right away, but keep reading until it grows on you.

If you get a smirk from your friends or family, just ignore them and keep doing what you're doing. They'll be amazed in the next few years. They will learn to understand and appreciate that you're not just having fun–you're building a real business.

When you're offered a telemarketing job at Oneida Silversmith's, take it! It's only $8 an hour, but you'll see your name on the list of "Top Performers" a lot. This will give you the confidence and financial support you'll need while building your business.

Before I forget, be sure to buy the "milana.com" domain name while you can still get it for $35–otherwise, you may have to pay $400 to some Korean guy who's holding it "hostage" a few years later.

After you spend one year learning about coaching, business and marketing, create ACCPOW. Starting the Association of Coaching & Consulting Professionals on the Web will be the first smart decision you'll make in your business. You might not know everything you need to know about coaching, but that's not the point. You'll know enough to interview successful coaches and business experts, and pass on what you learn to your members. In time, you'll become just as knowledgeable and experienced as the experts.

Here's the final piece of advice…

Even if you don't listen to anything I've just said, listen to this: no matter what you do, or how frustrated and scared you might feel, don't ever quit! Quitting is the only thing that will definitely prevent you from becoming wealthy. If you keep doing what you're doing, everything will be OK. Everything will fall into place, and you'll never have to worry about money or the financial future of your family again.

-- A Friend

Can You Really Make Millions in Coaching?

There are many skeptics who don't believe you can make a million dollars in coaching. Most of us are surrounded by people who trade hours for dollars and for whom the sound of "million dollars" seems unreal, almost cosmic. I used to think that millionaires were "superhumans" who simply made a deal with the almighty himself, and left everyone else in the dust.

The truth is, they're as real as anyone else—they simply operate on a bigger scale. They play in a bigger "sandbox." In every industry you can find a millionaire-coach. Do they spend their days coaching people one-on-one? Unlikely. What they do is follow these three core principles to take their business to a million-dollar level:

#1: Niche – they get really *really* good at something! They learn everything about a specific area of their expertise and a specific group of people, and focus on making money with what they're best at.

#2: Leverage – they leverage time, people, content, technology and other resources to automate and amplify everything they do.

#3: Create a Need for Coaching – millionaire-coaches don't sell coaching. They create a need for coaching through their products, programs, courses, seminars, events and other services.

Look at your business today. Do you use these principles in the most effective way possible? Every strategy I shared with you here is used by all "coaching millionaires" today in one way or another. Once you start using them, there will be no way of stopping your income growth. And that's how Coaching Millions are made!

Claim your free gift worth $147 at www.coachingmillions.com/gift

Exclusive Offer for the
Readers of This Book

"Make Money With Coaching"

COACHING SUCCESS KIT

If you are ready to start selling coaching or add coaching income to your existing business in the next 24-72 hours, this coaching success kit offers a great jump-start!

Here's what it includes:

- **18 Ways to Start Selling Coaching in the Next 24 Hours**

- **42 Things I Learned About Creating and Selling High-Priced Coaching and Mentorship Programs**

- **How to Create Your Own Lucrative Niche Coaching Programs**

Plus, if you order from the the special link below, I will include *9 expert panel discussions* on <u>coaching business building</u>, <u>business management</u> and <u>passive income</u>, which were I personally facilitated with some of the top coaching entrepreneurs in the world!

This offer is NOT available anywhere else:

www.makemoneywithcoaching.com/special

Where Do I Go From Here?

I truly believe that I am where I am today because I did everything I shared with you in this book. If you're thinking, "I'm also doing all the things you talk about and my business is nowhere near where I want it to be!"–Think again. I guarantee that if you look closely at what you do and how you do it, you'll find that you may have ignored or skipped a few important elements.

Let's recap.

Find a Niche

Don't underestimate the power of working within a niche. If you don't have a niche (specialty + target audience), you'll find yourself struggling or stuck–no matter what else you are doing right. If you're looking for more ideas on where to focus your attention, go online and search for "association" on Google.com. This will provide thousands of results on existing groups and associations–a sure way to identify your niche fast. If you're new to your target audience, don't worry: you'll only need to read a few magazines and attend a conference to understand their world. Of course, to *deeply* understand their issues and challenges, you'll need to spend more time reading, surveying and coaching a couple of clients.

Pick Your Coaching Model

Most of the world's people know nothing about coaching. But they *do* know what problem they need help in solving, or what goal they need help in reaching. Develop a coaching program or programs for your business, and then create a process to enroll clients. This might involve conducting free seminars or teleclasses a few weeks before your program starts. It could mean running an e-mail campaign or sending out physical letters to people in your network. Whatever method you choose to spread the word about your coaching, people need to understand and become excited about the results they'll see when they complete the program. Treat your coaching program like a product and you'll enroll more clients than you ever thought possible.

Build Your Presence

Once you've identified your market, it's time to announce your arrival. Start writing articles, conducting teleseminars, publishing a newsletter, and introducing yourself to the "players" in your industry. I began receiving many more "yes's" after creating an association–it was more real, more important, and more credible to people who'd never heard of me. Consider starting an online resource center, community, or training university to brand your company. You don't have be an expert to do this, but once you start working with clients and interviewing successful people in your target audience as a part of your research, you'll feel much more confident, knowledgeable, and ready to deliver big value.

Create Passive Coaching Income

Whether you love to coach clients, hold teleseminars, or lead live events, I'm sure you also love taking time off. But why stop making money when you're not coaching? Building passive income sources into your business gives you freedom by leveraging your knowledge. Everything you say is gold. Everything you write is gold. Everything you think is gold. Collect it, package it, bundle it, archive it–do whatever's necessary to create information products. Keep asking, "How can I turn one thing into something else: an article into an audio CD, an e-book into a home study course, a coaching program into a self-coaching system." My husband sometimes thinks that money literally falls into my lap. He doesn't see the work I put into setting things up, but I once I do, it continues to generate revenue whether I'm there or not. Also keep in mind that people associate authorship with expertise–if you wrote the book, you're an expert. Even if you weren't before, you are now.

Build a Self-Propelled Lifestyle Business

As the saying goes, "Success comes at a price." If you don't learn to manage it all, you'll notice a drop in your energy level, your income, and your quality of life. To create a business that works without you–or with minimal involvement, doing only the things you absolutely love–you need to trust others, and let them help you operate the business. The more comfortable you become with delegating, the faster you'll create a "turnkey" coaching business that works without you. The more trust you put in your team members, the emptier your "yuck bucket" will be, and the more you'll enjoy every day of your life.

Become a Leader in Your Field through Edge and Innovation

There is always one person who takes the lead–in life and in business. The leader creates, takes risks, speaks out, and pushes to the edge of what he believes. The rest follow. Who's the leader in your industry? Can it be you? Why not? If someone is already well known in your niche and considered a leader, take a look at what they're doing AND what they are *not* doing. What trends or problems are they ignoring? Could you be the one who develops solutions to fill the need? The best way to invent solutions is to survey your target audience, even interviewing some of them personally. Ask this question: "If you could have a magic wand and wish for anything, what would it be?" Be ready to take notes because the magic is about to happen!

Final Thoughts

As I was writing this book and asking people to review it, I heard the same thing over and over again. "Milana, where is all the information about networking, referrals, selling and closing techniques, and all the other traditional business building strategies?"

The truth is, I used none of the above methods in building a very thriving business. Instead, I followed the steps outlined in the book–from establishing a niche, discovering the needs of my target audience, creating products and programs, and finally, "penetrating" my niche with articles, events, teleseminars, and tools for success. Then clients came, as if effortlessly.

Why did it work?

First of all, thanks to modern technology–a combination of the Internet, telephone, and conference lines–I never had to set foot outside my home office.

Second, it suited my lifestyle. When I was in college, I had to commute almost 3 hours a day, six days a week for several years. I guess I developed a huge aversion to traveling–I love working from home! So I subconsciously designed my life and business to make sure I never have to travel. This required a lot of passive strategies to build my business. I have everything I need right in front of me–my computer, my telephone, my planner, my library, my office supplies. If I do need something, I can just go online and purchase it.

If you love getting out there, networking, speaking, creating connections, and it brings you results, then please continue to do so. If these activities have not worked for you, or you want to make your client attraction effortless, then follow the strategies in this book. It worked for me, it worked for hundreds of coaches who use these strategies, and it can work for you, too.

You will, however, need to be persistent and stop at nothing. If an idea or strategy didn't work for you in the past, it's most likely because you haven't given it a good try. I started up many things, which never turned into something big. Some might say that I failed in those things. I know that I simply didn't have enough passion to see them through to success. I quit before I could see the fruit of my labor.

By the way, you already know everything you need to know about success and how to achieve it. The question is, are you doing it? As Napoleon Hill said, knowledge is *not* power. It only becomes power when it's organized into a plan of action!

You also need a push, that final dose of inspiration, and someone to actually guide them through implementing it. I used to greatly underestimate the power of having a "cheerleader" and a support team in my life. I was determined to find my own answers. I struggled, I made a ton of mistakes, I even made a fool of myself a few times.

On my own, I did ok—well, probably, better than okay. But when I enrolled into a mastermind group and started working with a coach, things just sped up! I shortened my path! I started making huge leaps and achieving things I never dared to try before.

Get a coach or a mentor as soon as you're possibly able to. Join a mastermind support group—if you don't have one in your area, start one. It'll make a world of difference in every step you take.

To your extraordinary success,
Milana Leshinsky

Appendix A

Coaching Business Models Study

As part of my research for this book, I conducted a study to find out how coaches operate their business, what they struggle with, and what areas they need help with the most. Below, I present to you the results of my discoveries, compiled from the responses of 478 coaches from all over the world.

Coaching Business Survey

Conducted by ACCPOW,
Association of Coaching & Consulting Professionals on the Web
http://www.accpow.com .

Copyright © 2006, ACCPOW & Milana.com, LLC

EXECUTIVE SUMMARY

In June 2006, 478 coaches participated in a study conducted by ACCPOW, the Association of Coaching & Consulting Professionals on the Web. The purpose of the study was to learn about how coaches operate their businesses, what their business models look like, what challenges they are faced with, and what solutions they found that work. Several trends have been uncovered in analyzing the survey data. Almost half of the respondents said that they have fewer than five one-on-one coaching clients, while only 7% stated that they have more than twenty clients. One in ten participants reported that they have no paying clients at this time.

Over half of the participants do not offer any information products, and of those who do, the majority offer e-books, workbooks, and audio CDs. While most of the participants reported that they work in their businesses under 30 hours a week, almost 30% said that a day job, consulting, or second business is their primary source of income. Although the majority of respondents are aware of what virtual assistants do, only 21% of them actually use a virtual assistant in their coaching business. Coaching clients one-on-one is still the most important source of income, with only 16% of respondents involved in a more "passive" coaching model, such as coaching clubs or coaching "gyms."

1. How many information products do you sell?

54%	None Yet
22.9%	1-2
9.1%	3-4
12.4%	5+
3%	Other

2. Which of the following products do you offer?

42.8%	E-books
32.3%	Workbooks
36.0%	Assessments
22.9%	Audio CDs
22.9%	Books (in print)
24.6%	Special Reports
20.2%	Home-Study Courses
17.2%	Workbooks (in print)
10.8%	CDs (computer)

3. Which of the following paid continuity programs do you offer?

68.8%	Group Coaching
22.5%	Other
17.1%	Mastermind Peer Group
16.7%	Subscription Site
9.6%	Coaching Club
7.1%	Coaching Gym
5.4%	Paid Newsletter

4. How many one-on-one clients do you currently have?

10.9%	None yet
46.6%	1-5
20.2%	6-10
9.3%	11-15
4.3%	16-20
6.9%	21+
3.6%	Other

5. How many hours a week do you work in and on your coaching business, total?

35.6%	15-20
20.3%	20-30
16.2%	30-40
10.7%	40-50
6.5%	50+
11.9%	Other

6. What is your biggest source of income?

53.4%	Individual Coaching Clients
29.7%	Other

7.4%	Group Coaching
4.4%	Information Products
2.7%	Speaking
2.5%	Subscription Site

7. Do you currently work with a Virtual Assistant?

21.3%	Yes
66.4%	No
12.3%	No idea what this means

The most frequently mentioned concerns of coaches included:

Finding clients
Lack of marketing knowledge
Most people still can't afford coaching
The majority of people still don't "get" the benefits of coaching
Getting steady income
Differentiating myself from other coaches
Lack of help in getting started
Too many coaches in the world today

Appendix B

Is Your Product or Service an "Ideavirus?"

By Milana Leshinsky

"Unleashing the Ideavirus" by Seth Godin is one of the most important books on business and marketing. It is not about finding the right marketing strategies or knowing the right places to advertise in. It's about creating a remarkable product with the marketing built right into the product!

The concept behind the Ideavirus is NOT making as much money as you can with your product right away–a different strategy would need to be in place for this. The concept is to spread the word about your product or service to as many people in the world as possible, then leverage your audience by selling a paid version of this product or a completely different product.

For example, WinZip used to offer a free version of their file compression software for years. Last month I checked their site, and the free version is no longer available. But guess what! This program has become so popular among Windows users; it's almost a standard! Who cares about paying $30 for it now, if you "can't live" without it!

The same thing is happening to many other products. The Internet is making things happen so much faster and easier today. It "amplifies" the word-of-mouth by thousands!

Do you have a product or service that's an ideavirus? Could it become one with a few tweaks? Take this quiz to find out: www.assessmentgenerator.com/ideavirus_assessment.html

Ideavirus Self-Assessment

Check each box that truthfully applies to you, and find out whether your product or service has a potential of being an "Ideavirus."

- ❑ I am the first one to introduce this idea.
- ❑ Nobody would ever call my product boring.
- ❑ There is a free trial available.
- ❑ The trial/demo is fast and painless.
- ❑ There is literally no learning curve in using the product.
- ❑ There is an existing audience for this product.
- ❑ There are 3 or more magazines already being published specifically for this audience.
- ❑ My product is easy to understand and can be explained in one simple sentence.
- ❑ It can be easily shared with others without too much hassle.
- ❑ People get excited about using my product.
- ❑ Customers can use my product over and over again.
- ❑ My product can be called at least one of these adjectives: cool, remarkable, thought-provoking, funny, important, impressive, profit generating.
- ❑ I can continue introducing new products for the same audience to leverage the customer base I build with this product.
- ❑ I have an affiliate program in place to reward my 'sneezers' for spreading the word about my product. An affiliate program simply allows me to track the sales my joint venture partners help me generate.
- ❑ I have put together text ads, articles, and letters my affiliates can use to spread the word.
- ❑ The more people use my product, the more other people learn about it. In other words, my product carries a promotional message inside of it. (For example, every email

sent via Hotmail has a message at the bottom of it: 'Get your own free email account from Hotmail').

❑ My product impresses people.

❑ My product has an exciting look, feel, and image (e.g., high-impact web site, unique logo design, etc.).

❑ Letting others know about my product makes people feel smart and special.

12- Step Action Plan for Becoming a Successful Coaching Entrepreneur

"It's all theory until you do it!"

I hope that reading "Coaching Millions" has shifted the way you think about your business, your time, and your lifestyle. But, as coaches, both you and I know that simply reading it will not make you a successful coaching entrepreneur. You need to implement what you learned.

That's why I am including a 12-Step action plan for you to implement. The results of following these Steps will vary based on your niche, your background, and the level of your persistence. You can use this action plan with your own coach, by enrolling into my coaching club, or by yourself. Regardless of how you do it, it's important that you get into action right now. I've given you the tools - your success is in your hands!

Step 1: Determine Your Niche

Step 2: Create Your Coaching Habitat

Step 3: Study Your Market

Step 4: Design a Free Offer

Step 5: Create a Lead Generating Mini-Site

Step 6: Publish an Article

Step 7: Create a Product

Step 8: Create a Mini-Site to Sell Your Product

Step 9: Develop a Coaching Program

Step 10: Generate Coaching Leads

Step 11: Fill Your Coaching Program

Step 12: Design Your Lifestyle

Step1: Determine Your Niche

The first Step in determining your niche is identifying your skills and passions. Write down your answers to these questions:

- *If you could do something all day long, what would it be?*

- *If you were told to write a "how-to" book in a week, what subject would you choose?*

- *If you had to write a series of 12 booklets, what topics would they include, and what would link them together?*

- *What are some of your past careers?*

- *What jobs do your friends and family members hold?*

- *What obstacle(s) have you successfully overcome, and how?*

- *Which of your life experiences could others learn from?*

Based on your answers, list three to five possible target markets that may be interested in what you have to offer. Use this checklist to find out which target market has the greatest potential for your business:

- ❑ This group of people has specialized interests and needs.
- ❑ They have a strong desire for what you offer.

- ❏ You can easily reach individual prospects within the group.
- ❏ The group is large enough to produce the volume of business you need.
- ❏ The group is small enough that your competition is likely to overlook it.
- ❏ You are, or used to be, a part of this group of people.
- ❏ Your target prospects are in the financial position to afford your products and services.
- ❏ You enjoy working with people in this niche.
- ❏ You can see yourself creating various products and services to offer to your niche market.

Identify your niche based on your results.

Step 2: Create Your Coaching Habitat

Once you identified your niche, it's important to understand your "coaching habitat"—an environment in which you will be focusing your marketing efforts and connecting with clients and partners. Write down the answers to these questions:

#1: Your Background (Soil).

What background do you have that relates to your target audience?

#2: Specialized Interests (Defined Borders).

What specialized interests and needs do members of your target audience share?

#3: Market Accessibility (Water).

What associations, organizations, and publications exist for your target audience?

#4: Growth Potential (Sun & Space).

What events happen in your chosen industry? What historical data and predictions have been made about this industry by related organizations?

#5: Coaching Issues (Food).

What are the top 3-5 issues and challenges within your specialty your target audience needs help with?

#6: Colleagues and Competitors (Existing Vegetation).

What are the top 3-5 coaches that offer the same or similar services to your target audience? What makes you different?

#7: Marketing Strategies (Planting Time).

What is your target audience's preferred method of consuming information? What observations have you made about how they think, operate and communicate?

#8: Lifestyle and Habits (Traffic Patterns).

What have you observed about your target audience's lifestyle, goals, and values? Do you feel comfortable with what you discovered?

Step 3: Study Your Market

This week's objective is to get familiar with your target audience on a deeper level.

1. Subscribe to 3-5 online newsletters published specifically for your target audience.

2. Explore 2-3 books published in your chosen field of expertise.

3. Interview at least 5 members of your target audience in person or on the telephone.

- *What kind of books or magazines do you buy?*

- *What are your biggest challenges?*

- *What does a typical day look like for you?*

- *What recently discovered product or service really excites you?*

- *What was the most expensive product or service you ever bought?*

- *What are the top three things you'd like to accomplish in the next 6 months?*

- *What's not working? What are you doing over and over again without the desired results?*

For more interview question ideas, go to "30 Questions to Ask Your Target Audience" section in Part II, Getting Rich in the Niche.

4. Search the Internet for existing programs, products, services, and solutions offered in your field. Your purpose is to observe and discover what is already offered, what may be missing from the existing solutions, and how you can brand yourself in a unique way. As you are conducting this research, keep a file of all resources you discover. Newsletters, membership web sites, organizations, non-competing professionals, vendors who target the same audience, message boards, discussion forums, and potential joint venture partners are what you want to have on your list by the time you're done with your research.

Step 4: Design a Free Offer

Creating a free offer will help you build your mailing list and give you a way of turning prospects into customers. Ask yourself these two questions:

1. *If I were to pick the most important challenge members of my target audience experience and are frustrated by, what would it be?*

2. *If I were to pick the most important goal members of my target audience want to achieve and are willing to do anything to get it, what would it be?*

Based on your answers, create a special report, an e-course, an audio mini-course, or any other educational report that:

- Is highly relevant to your target audience;

- Helps them solve an immediate problem;

- Is something they can't easily find elsewhere;

- Has a high-perceived value.

Be sure to include information about your coaching program in the free giveaway. For more details on designing an effective free offer, re-read the section titled "Make Them an Offer They Can't Refuse" in Part IV: Building Your Market Presence.

Step 5: Create a Lead Generating Mini-Site

Don't just give away your special report–ask for a name and an e-mail address first. For this purpose, you'll need to create a one-page web site that will contain two things:

1. "Sales" copy–a brief but highly enticing explanation of what you're giving away and why they should absolutely have it. Even though it's free, you still need to show your visitors what it can help them achieve or overcome. I highly recommend getting a separate domain name for this mini-site, because you'll be referring to it a lot in your other materials.

2. Opt-in form–a sign-up form, which asks for their name and e-mail address, and allows your prospects to receive the special report they requested. This can be accomplished by getting an account with an auto responder service. I recommend several such services in the book resources center.

Step 6: Publish an Article

The first article written for your niche must be your BEST article. It has to be highly useful, practical, well written, and easily understandable. Most importantly, it has to be highly relevant to your target audience and preferably on a controversial topic. Write an article with one of these angles:

- "How to…"

- "Top 10 Secrets to…"

- "33 Ways to…"

…Or any other angle you can have to make your article invaluable to the publisher of an industry newsletter or magazine. Your article should be about 800 words (not too short, not too long) to be "picked up" by just about any interested publisher. When you're done, submit your article to newsletter editors, article submission web sites, and article depositories. You can find a large list of such sites in the book resources center. In my experience, though, hand picking the places and people to submit your articles to is the most effective strategy. It allows you to target and customize your

submissions a lot better.

Step 7: Create a Product

To penetrate your niche, it's important to establish yourself as an expert. The easiest way to demonstrate your expertise is coming out with a product in your specialty, which is highly relevant to your target audience.

Use one of these ideas to create your product:

1. Record yourself answering questions that were generated as a result of your research. Transcribe it and turn into an audio CD + transcript product.

2. Look through the existing materials, articles, tips, and e-mails you sent to people in response to their questions. There is most likely a wealth of information ready to be turned into a product.

3. Create a series of special reports (or record them as a series of audio segments) based on 6-12 of the most important topics in your industry.

4. Expand the article or special report you created earlier into a more comprehensive product, with examples, resources, and case studies from your research.

5. If you're very new to your niche, conduct a series of interviews with experts (written or recorded) on some of the "hottest" topics in your industry.

For more ideas and details on developing an information product, re-read the section called "Creating Your First Product" in Part V, Passive Coaching Income.

Step 8: Create a Mini-Site to Sell Your Information Product

Just like with a free giveaway, you need a separate web site to sell your information product. Remember that a product-selling site should only have one purpose–to sell your product. For that reason, you need a powerful and compelling letter inviting prospects to buy. For details on creating an effective "sales letter," re-read the section called "Creating a No-Brainer Offer" in Part IV: Pick Your Coaching Model. Also, consider hiring a professional copywriter to help you write an enticing sales letter. It might cost you a few hundred dollars, but it will pay off many times over.

At this point, you should also have a shopping cart set up to sell your product. The best shopping cart service also comes with unlimited auto responders, customer database, and many other important features you'll use in your business. I recommend such a service in the book resources center.

Step 9: Develop a Coaching Program

A coaching program will serve as the "back-end" offers to any products, teleseminars, articles or live seminars you'll be putting together. A good coaching program has a step-by-step process for achieving a specific goal.

Follow these steps to create your own coaching program:

1. Choose the model that fits your preferences, goals and your lifestyle (coaching gym, coaching club, inner circle, introductory program, step-by-step program, action plan program, mastermind program, virtual coaching program, training, or certification program, etc.).

2. Come up with the central topic and outline your program's content.

3. Add any relevant tools, bonuses, and resources to make your program more valuable.

4. Decide how to price your program based on the end results it delivers, the time and energy you'll be putting into running it, and the pricing your target audience is comfortable with.

5. Write a "sales letter" to explain your coaching program and create a one-page web site to enroll participants.

For more details on creating an effective coaching program that will sell, re-read Part IV, Pick Your Coaching Model.

Step 10: Generate Coaching Leads

Now that you have a web site, an opt-in form, a free giveaway, a product, and a coaching program in place, it's time to start generating leads! Here are the two strategies I have found that bring the best results:

1. Offer a free teleseminar based on your special report. You can do so by contacting companies, organizations, and newsletter publishers who target the same audience as you. You may also want to turn your article into a hard copy printout and send it out to highly targeted organizations, companies and managers. It's important to follow up. One e-mail or mailing is not enough to close the deal. *Your goal is to get these companies to announce your free teleseminar to their members and customers.*

2. Write and submit an article. It has to be your BEST article ever, because you'll want every online newsletter publisher, magazine editor, and membership site owner who targets your audience to publish it for their readers. Your article should be provocative, controversial, trendy, funny, insightful, personal, and whatever else you think is important to "touch" your audience. You should also submit it to online article directories and discussion lists (see specific places to submit in the book resources center). Of course, remember to include a resource box that points to your free giveaway web site. For more details, re-read the *Writing Articles to Bring Coaching Leads section* in Part III.

If you use both of these strategies, you should start getting dozens of leads daily in your database. But you must be persistent, especially when it comes to contacting companies–even if it means outsourcing this to your assistant.

Step 11: Fill Your Coaching Program

To fill your program with clients successfully, you need to think of this as an enrollment campaign – a focused, consistent, time-defined set of actions that motivate prospects to sign up. Here are the five strategies you need to use to ensure that your program fills up fast:

1. **Sales letter site**–this is the most important element of your enrollment campaign. Refer back to *Creating a No-Brainer Offer* section in Part IV of the book to develop an effective enrollment letter for your coaching program.

2. **E-Mail Announcements**–a series of consistent e-mail "teasers" that both educate and invite people to your program will dramatically help you increase your enrollment. Each announcement should be a combination of an article and a promotion.

3. **Hold a free teleseminar for your mailing list**–connecting with prospects, explaining your program, and inviting them to enroll is very important. Alex Mandossian, the author of *Teleseminar Secrets*, calls it "marketing intimacy" because they get to hear your voice and get to know, like and trust you faster than through any other medium (other than TV, perhaps). Announce your teleseminar once you have a list of at least 80-100 highly targeted prospects, and invite them join you. I found a lot of success with free teleseminars, but you can achieve similar results with live workshops.

4. **"Early Bird" Specials**–to reward early decision makers, I highly recommend either giving them a discount or adding a special bonus when they enroll by a certain date. I've given a 25% discount, a free audio CD with case studies, and even access to my personal "Rolodex" as an "early-bird" special. What would your clients appreciate as a bonus? You can announce your "early-bird" bonus as a separate mailing,

during a free teleseminar, or in a P.S. section of your e-mail announcements.

5. **Ask your joint venture partners and affiliates to announce your program**–you can't do it alone, nor should you attempt to. You can accelerate your sign-ups with just a single JV partner who said, "YES" to you. To make it more attractive to your joint venture partners, you may invite them to be guest speakers in your program, give them a plug during your calls, or even make them a sponsor on your web site. It's key to understand what motivates them to act–for more ideas on how to build a relationship with JV partners, re-read *My Recipe for Joint Venture Success* section in Part III.

Step 12: Design Your Lifestyle

As you build your business, create products, and attract clients, you want to keep a close eye on how your lifestyle is affected by all of these transformations. Remember, your goal is not to create a full-time job for yourself–it's to create a business that will support the lifestyle of your dreams.

Don't allow yourself to say, "I'd love to have that, but that's probably unrealistic." If you want to work two hours a day, then design your days in the way that allow you to do that.

I purposely keep my one-on-one client count low so that I can have plenty of free time and work on my own projects. I also delegate a lot to my assistants. Even if it means increasing my costs, as long as I am able to spend time with my kids and keep my "yuck bucket" empty, it is worth it to me.

Who's to say you can't do it? Decide what you want and do it! But to have a lot of free time and flexibility, you must have certain elements in place.

1. Automate your systems

Look through your marketing strategies - lead generation, follow-up, screening, enrollment, etc. - and make sure every aspect of it is automated wherever possible. Very little of your marketing should be done manually. Once you have a client enrolled, then you can deliver personalized service.

Many actions can be automated using an auto responder, a web-based program that sends automatic messages when triggered. You can also automate delivery or your information products to customers using a combination of an auto responder and a shopping cart.

You don't need to do this all by yourself. In fact, your virtual assistant can do all this. This way you don't have to get involved into the technical details and logistics of running your business. Leave it to the pros.

2. Build your "dream team"

Speaking of pros, it's important to build a team of professionals who can support you. Start by creating your personal activity grid, illustrated in part VI, a self-propelled business in the "painting yourself into a corner" section. Take a look at what activities fall under the second and third column: things you can do yourself, but could easily be done by someone else and things you don't know how (or want to know how) to do. Then determine who could be doing these things for you and bring these people into your "dream team."

The first person you need to hire is a virtual assistant - all administrative and customer support issues can be handled by a VA.

3. Complete a product funnel (or a "Coaching Diamond™")

A product funnel will allow you to have an almost effortless client enrollment process in your business. Map out your product funnel to see where each product or program falls. What's missing in your funnel? How can you quickly create an offer to fill the gap?

Make sure that your product funnel follows these 3 important rules:

- Every item has to have a "back-end" product.

- Offer more low-cost products than high-priced products.

- At least one product in the funnel should generate recurring income.

4. Create a continuity program

A continuity program is simply a way to support your clients after they purchase your product or go through your program. It usually lasts at least 6 months (in some cases for years). For example, a group program in the "coaching gym" format may go on for 12 months. An inner circle type program might last indefinitely, for as long as members receive value and enjoy being a part of it.

The best way to start a continuity, or continuing education program, is to ask yourself these questions:

- *How can I support my clients after they've purchased all my products and have gone through my seminars?*

- *What problems do my products create for clients that can be solved with additional support?*

Re-read the section on subscription sites in Part V: Passive Coaching Income, to get more ideas for making your continuity program much more valuable for your clients. Also, take a look at the Coaching Diamond model introduced in the same chapter, and think about how it can be applied to your business.

About the Author

Milana Leshinsky is an entrepreneur, author, and business advisor to independent professionals.

Originally from Ukraine, Milana spent most of her life studying to become a music teacher. Having attended a music school since the age of eight, in 1988, she entered into *Gliera,* one of the most prestigious music colleges in the former Soviet Union. Milana spent the next four years majoring in the history and theory of music. She graduated in the spring of 1992.

Shortly thereafter, Milana and her family immigrated to the United States, where she planned to continue her music education by enrolling in a local college in Syracuse, New York. To her surprise, the music education system in America proved to be very different and she quickly switched to another major.

In 1998, Milana graduated with a Bachelor's degree in Computer Information Systems, and spent the next three years working as a programmer and a web developer for several companies in New York and Pennsylvania.

In 2000, Milana discovered the world of Internet Marketing. In attempt to become a work-at-home mom, she quit her job and launched an Internet-based business.

After writing and successfully selling three digitally published books, Milana was introduced to coaching. In 2002, she founded the *Association of Coaching & Consulting Professionals on the Web (ACCPOW),* a place for coaches to learn and acquire the tools for building a global business. Milana also runs annual global *Coaching Telesummit,* which she pioneered in 2005.

You can visit her on the web at www.milana.com.

Other Valuable Resources from Milana Leshinsky

Coaching Millions System: The Ultimate Lifestyle Business Success System

If you are ready to become the leading coaching expert in your industry, generate six to seven figures, and be a successful lifestyle entrepreneur, this system is everything you'll need. It will take you *step-by-step through implementing the six building blocks introduced in the book* and show you dozens of shortcuts you won't find anywhere else.
http://www.coachingmillions.com/system

Coaching Membership Web Site Secrets

To generate predictable monthly source of income that accumulates and grows over time, you can build your coaching club, coaching "gym" or another type of coaching membership web site. *This is how you really build a million-dollar coaching business - through creating a continuity program.* Everything you want to know about building a successful membership web site is packaged inside this product, including interviews with 7-figure entrepreneurs who run their own coaching clubs and "gyms."
www.membershipwebsitesecrets.com

Coaching Millionaire in Training

If you are ready to take your business into the big leagues, become a niche leader, and earn multi-six figures in coaching, I am inviting you to check out my exclusive coaching club, Coaching Millionaire in Training. This is the only place where I don't hold anything back and give you my best strategies and advice. I also *interview one highly successful entrepreneur every month* so you never run out of creative marketing and lifestyle ideas in your coaching business!
www.coachingmillionaireintraining.com

Index